From the Outer

From the Outer

Footy like you've never heard it

Edited by Alicia Sometimes and Nicole Hayes

Published by Black Inc.,
an imprint of Schwartz Publishing Pty Ltd
Wurundjeri Country
22-24 Northumberland Street
Collingwood VIC 3066, Australia
enquiries@blackincbooks.com
www.blackincbooks.com

First published 2016; reprinted 2019, 2023

9781863958288 (paperback)
9781925203899 (ebook)

A catalogue record for this book is available from the National Library of Australia

Cover artwork by Oslo Davis; design by Peter Long
Text design and typesetting by Tristan Main

Printed in Australia by McPherson's Printing Group.

For my dad, Geoffrey William Hayes, for showing me the poetry in football, and the power in words.

Nicole Hayes

For my dad, Gary, the long-suffering Saints supporter who wonders where he went wrong by having a little Hawker in the family.

Alicia Sometimes

CONTENTS

INTRODUCTION

Alicia Sometimes & Nicole Hayes

We've always loved footy – huddled amongst the screaming fans, scratching stats into the Record, playing kick-to-kick on the oval, or watching the replay for the sixteenth time. Footy is how we met. We are both former (frustrated) players who hark back to a time when girls weren't allowed to play, yet stealing every minute of game time sympathetic coaches would allow us. And today, both diehard Hawthorn fans (don't judge us!), suffering the team's losses and celebrating their wins with the same passion that drove us to want to play all those years ago.

Always, though, it's been about the game itself. Bigger than any team, or any individual. A story so all encompassing, it seems never to grow old. A story that is slowly changing.

This was the thing that drove us to develop this anthology. Despite the breadth and influence of AFL on our culture, there were so many voices not being heard, so many possibilities left unexplored. We were determined to change this.

The idea was to wrest the conversation around footy from the usual suspects and hand the microphone over to those writers with something new to say, in an attempt to explain our often complex but still deeply felt relationship with the game.

There are so many fans with diverse or disadvantaged backgrounds, whether through gender, culture, geography, disability, sexuality or the socio-economic. But too often we don't hear from them. In seeking out untold stories, we've tried to broaden the conversation to reflect the extent of this diversity.

These stories are, for the most part, love letters to footy. But as with many love affairs, the sting of disappointment and betrayal can be more potent, more poignant, than the heady rush of love. For some, it was enough to drive them away. But for others, it's more complicated. So we have tried to capture the moment or memory that has stayed with us, the spark that resonated most, from the perspective of those who love the game even when the game hasn't always loved them.

People like Peta Searle, the first woman to coach at a senior level; Leila Gurruwiwi, a founding member of the first Indigenous footy show; and Chelsea Roffey, the first female goal umpire to officiate at an AFL grand final; Bev O'Connor, the first female vice president of a club, and Jason Tuazon-McCheyne, the founding member of the Purple Bombers, an LGBTI-friendly cheer squad. And writers who are rarely asked to write about this game they love but have plenty to say. These are the people whose stories we wanted to hear.

We wanted to celebrate the changes, too: the promise of a Women's League in 2017; the first Rainbow Round in 2016; the rapidly expanding number of girls playing footy – the fastest growing sporting community in the country; the resilience of the regional game; the teams for those with physical and mental disabilities; the Community Cup; the recognition of our multicultural heritage … These stories need to be told.

Finally, we wanted to challenge the notion that loving football is somehow anti-intellectual. To show that it doesn't have to be either/or in the arts-versus-sport discourse. In fact, it shouldn't even be a competition. *From the Outer* draws on both of these cultural institutions – the literary and the sporting – celebrating this uniquely Australian game by bringing together an incredible array of talented writers and storytellers who have enthralled us, entertained us and made us think. We hope you enjoy reading this collection as much as we loved putting it together.

AN OPEN LETTER TO DOUBTING THOMAS

Chelsea Roffey

Dear Thomas,

Where has the time gone? The past decade as an AFL umpire has flown, and there's one question that continues to surface, second only to 'Are you allowed to date the players?' The question is: 'What barriers have you faced as a female in a male domain?'

Where do I start? To be frank, when I reflect on the hardships of gender, it's difficult to believe I survived this long – I've faced more hurdles than Sally Pearson! The intrinsic differences of gender have created a myriad of challenges to overcome. Biology, as you have so insightfully observed, has made an indelible mark.

Some airheads, like the respected neuroscientist and writer Cordelia Fine, suggest that gender stereotypes are not biologically hardwired at all, but are the result of priming based on social expectations. However, like you, I find detailed 'empirical evidence' hard to swallow, especially when it is so clumsily wrapped up in the guise of 'neuro-endocrinological investigation'. In more sensible times, assertions like this would have got you burnt at the stake.

Let me elaborate by addressing the elephant in the room. Women are, quite literally, girls. Everyone knows the top two things that don't belong on the footy field are girls and wusses (interchangeable, really). That's not to say they don't have their uses. There's nothing like a hardworking Aussie sheila expressing her God-given talents running the canteen or removing stubborn stains from twenty-two smelly guernseys every week. But girls on the field? It's a concept that undermines the fabric upon which this great nation is built. Ladies nurture and men make decisions – it's the law of nature.

As a baby of the '80s, there was one thing I noticed that a truly decisive man, a real man, wore with absolute pride: a moustache. Back then a man without a moustache was practically a woman in pants. All the men I loved had a moustache. What was intrepid filmmaker Alby Mangles, irresistible to the ladies and the ultimate man's man, without a mop of golden locks offset by an unkempt spray of whiskers? We looked to the mo when Merv Hughes and David Boon faced down England on the cricket pitch (or rose to the challenge of sinking a rumoured fifty-two beers on the plane flight over). Try imagining footy greats Ron

Barassi, Leigh Matthews and Malcolm Blight without one. My own father rocked a mo. And so it made perfect sense that a moustache on a goal umpire exuded the utmost authority. It was as much a part of the game as meat pies and yelling 'Ball!' for holding decisions. Though times had changed by the time I arrived on the AFL scene, my lack of facial hair was merely a clue to the underlying inadequacies that would be revealed in time.

The moustache situation would turn out to be the least of my worries.

There's the issue of not having played the game. I can still remember my first umpires' training session – I was transfixed by the silky-smooth football skills of the goal umpires as we replicated game-day scenarios. People tend to think umpires aren't good players, but it's time to blow that stereotype out of the water. Deciding who will play full-forward during our skills sessions is virtually impossible, they're all that good. We often invite our boss, Wayne Campbell, and ex-St Kilda captain Lenny Hayes, who does some part-time work with the AFL, to be the 'kickers' – mainly so they don't feel left out. Wayne jumps at the opportunity, being a former Richmond Tigers skipper and All-Australian, but he gets a thorough coaching clinic from our blokes.

Hence the trepidation for me, a female, who has never actually played a proper game! All I managed in my youth was the occasional kick-to-kick with Dad and my two brothers. As a spectator I excelled, religiously attending games since toddlerhood. And I was glued to the TV screen every time the mercurial talents of Tony Modra were on display. With time, I wrapped my lady brain around the mathematics of scoring, which naively gave me the idea I could handle the flag-waving for the teams at high school, even though I hadn't played. I later discovered that the first lesson you learn at umpiring school is to attach a printout of the six times tables to your scorecard. This enabled a raft of girls to join up, because as you know, all girls are bad at maths.

Dealing with hormones and emotions can be a rollercoaster for the fairer sex at the best of times, but overcoming the effects of oestrogen on game day, when maintaining focus is crucial, is no walk in the park. Female football fans are intrigued to learn how I maintain peak concentration in a testosterone-fuelled environment, amid a sea of short shorts, glistening biceps and guy-on-guy action. Not only must I read the flight and drop of the football to ensure precision in positioning to get the best view, but often I must jostle with half a dozen players milling around the goal area. I can literally smell the liniment evaporating off their muscles! At other times, my line of vision is interrupted by a rock-hard rump, not metres away, as a fullback reaches down to stretch a hamstring – and it's all I can do not to drool, open-mouthed. But nothing says 'Hello, ladies!' like a cheeky scratch to the groin, or a bushman's hanky, which involves blocking one nostril so the other can act as a chute for evacuating nasal congestion (ugly when it goes wrong). Men are remarkably at ease with their bodies, aren't they?

Asserting my authority has presented as another major challenge. When things get rowdy and a bit of elbow-lifting escalates to chest-bumping, it's mesmerising to watch, like having a window to a different species in its natural habitat. So primal. But monitoring this behaviour is vital, lest I wish to find myself attending a tribunal appearance to follow up a striking report. I can't just call on the nearest field umpire to rescue the situation; girl or not, I have a job to do. As you might imagine, reasoning with Fraser Gehrig when he's got his opponent in a headlock is a bit like trying to wrestle a bone from the mouth of a Doberman – you need to proceed with extreme caution.

In my case, channelling the voice and stern words of a mother brandishing the wooden spoon has been a successful tactic. But some people are so difficult to please. After reporting Barry Hall for wrestling with his opponent one day, I copped flack from a journalist who insisted I should have 'intervened'. On reflection, the vision of Hall knocking out Brent Staker with a single blow to the chin during another match must have been clouding my judgement. Any reasonable man would have stepped in, and if only I'd had the balls to place myself in the middle of a volatile situation, I would have been applauded for my courage.

I like to think being on the end of a few knocks and bumps is a sign that I've made it as an umpire, that the players treat me like any other 'white maggot' out on the field. But being typically clumsy (hormones, again!) can be problematic when you're faced with the decision to hold your ground behind the flight of the ball as Jonathan Brown rushes at you with the force of a steam train. Other highlights include the painful scrape of Todd Goldstein's size-14 football boot down the length of my shin during his run-up to a contest, and having my face connect with the end of a trademark Drew Petrie spoil. Occasionally I find myself standing in the goals next to Aaron Sandilands' hip and marvel at not being used as a speckie stepladder more often. But if you can't handle a 194-centimetre, 93-kilogram athlete lodging his knees in the back of your neck (thanks, Jarrad Waite!), being drilled with footies kicked from close range, the odd falcon, or seeing stars after spectators return the ball via the back of your head, get back to the kitchen, right?

I suppose you're wondering what sense of misguided confidence landed me here in the first place. I blame this one squarely on my parents for raising a daughter with self-worth and aspiration. I was encouraged to think big, and was impatient to achieve what I set my mind to. 'Four going on twenty-four,' Dad used to quip, which may explain the photo of me at the tender age of two, triumphantly clutching the perfect pot of beer I'd poured from the bar of the family's pub. A right little lady, I clomped around wearing my nanna's high heels and strings of beads from the op shop, appearing at the dinner table to sip from a water-filled wine glass, painted pinkie finger extended from the stem.

I loved dancing and performing. The *Grease* VHS was on high rotation in our house, but my favourite movie was *Dirty Dancing*, and Baby's winning attitude made a lasting impression. My favourite scene, to this day, is when she puts herself forward to step in as Johnny's dance partner, and he lays down the gauntlet: 'She can't do it. She cannot do it.' Baby narrows her eyes, purses her lips and shoots invisible daggers at him, as if to say, 'Screw. You.' (And she does exactly that, in more ways than one.) That's the moment where her infatuation is joined by self-respect and you know she's going to prove this gorgeous moron wrong and win his heart in the process.

Mum insists I was born with 'fear of missing out', which encouraged me to try new things. The potential for failure would always play second fiddle to FOMO. I still remember the part it played in my first regret. I was at the circus, aged three, when the acrobats called for a volunteer to climb into a harness and join the show. A huge spotlight moved across the sawdusted floor and over the crowd, landing on me. I froze. Despite desperately wanting to jump up and say, 'Yes! I'll do it!' I shyly shook my head. The pang of regret I felt as the opportunity passed was instant.

I attacked my first 'competition' – an apple-bobbing contest at age five – with gusto, leaving me drenched to the waist, but victorious. At twelve, I jumped head-first into a swollen creek during a cross-country event to leave competitors in my wake and secure a place in the state championships. By adolescence, I was getting good at feeling out of my depth. I'd travelled overseas on a tour of Asia, playing clarinet with the Queensland Symphonic Wind Orchestra, and I'd survived the public humiliation of an ear-wrenching vocal solo as Tallulah in my high school production of *Bugsy Malone*. From athletics and swimming carnivals to school exams, musical eisteddfods to debating, I spent a great deal of time channelling nerves in various activities. It would prove to be fantastic training for the pressure cooker of a full MCG crowd, having every move televised.

One of the greatest challenges of being elevated to the ranks of AFL has been navigating a 'no vulnerability' zone. The outward appearance of strength is rarely wrapped up in a feminine blanket, so proving you know your stuff in a man's sport takes extra effort. Breaking down in tears or storming off the field in a huff when things don't go your way aren't exactly hallmarks of composure, so it's essential to cultivate a hardened exterior. People often query whether I practise my signals in front of a mirror. 'No, of course not!' I inevitably lie, but in truth I devote weekly sessions to looking at my reflection, repeating 'Who's the man?' before slamming down a goal signal and shouting 'I am!'

Managing the princess persona ladies are inclined to adopt is tricky. If a woman can't indulge the pressures of body image, is she really a woman at all? I feel naked without nail polish and full make-up, but that's the price you pay for professionalism. Fortunately there's a hat to hide under! Initially I thought the cameras would be my biggest concern, with the weight they add, but the real task has been maintaining sex appeal in a pair of men's slacks and an oversized polo. You should see some of the clown pants I've been issued. Not to mention the ghastly silhouette created by the vest beneath my shirt, housing technology for an earpiece and a keypad for communicating decisions to the third scorer (difficult to avoid appearance of nipple-tweaking here). Then there's a head camera to capture anything the other fifty-three angles may have missed.

Even throwbacks to the old way of doing things presents challenges. I'll never forget Heritage Round, when I was issued with a coat, men's size XL. I loved the concept of the old-school uniform, but it made me look like the Stay Puft Marshmallow Man from *Ghostbusters*. Thankfully, Mum can sew, and having received the coat a day before my game, she lopped a chunk off each sleeve and a good 40 centimetres off the hem and reassembled the shoulders, taking care to conserve the 'PlayStation' sponsors' logo on the back.

Getting the outfit right is half the battle. Then there's the perpetual feminist issue that you, Thomas, brought to my attention: wearing appropriate underwear. This was a toughie. Those first few games as a professional AFL umpire were nerve-wracking and hugely exciting – being a lifelong footy fan who'd dedicated five and a half years to learning the skills of goal umpiring, reaching the pinnacle was a dream come true. All that training and preparation had led to this moment, and I was methodical in ensuring my equipment was in order. Boots, socks, pants, belt, top, hat, flags, scorecards, pens, coin, sunnies … I mentally ticked them off before heading onto the field and my pre-match jitters gave way to the hum of 30,000 fans in the Gabba stands. But there was something crucial I'd left off my list, that you politely reminded me of from over the fence at those early matches. Was I wearing my G-string?

As far as I knew, none of my colleagues wore jockstraps, and the AFL didn't give any direction around panties, so I assumed that comfortable underwear was the safest bet (we've all seen the stir Tania Buckley's jewel-encrusted G-string caused at the Brownlows). In the end, I went with a sensible pair that, truth be told, rivalled the knickers

Renée Zellweger made famous in *Bridget Jones' Diary*. How often can you say vanity loses out to practicality? If you're female, not very often – I guess I really am a pioneer! While we're on the topic, was it you who tossed the sizeable pair of jocks into the goal square one evening as I inspected the area, pre-game? If so, I hope you didn't sustain any chafing injuries!

Those who regard footy as a religion are familiar with the gospel of the cheer squad. Praise be, Thomas; these folks speak *the truth*. Like the time the man who routinely bursts my eardrums with profanities once admitted: 'I'm just a nice, normal guy, you know.' Rational advice regarding whether or not I've made the correct decision is always gratefully received – it's amazing how accurately people can assess super-tight scoring scenarios from all the way back in their seats. Their observations remain razor sharp, even after several beers! And clever? Sometimes I hear something so original, I commit it to memory. Like one time when I signalled a goal, and that chap yelled: 'How big is it?!', alluding to the size of my (absent) male genitalia. Classic! Mobile phone numbers called across the fence as I write down the score are appreciated, and I always record them to my contacts list post-game. Big ticks to the Romeo who complimented me on the switch to green uniforms ('You look great in lime green. I'd love to squeeze the juice out of ya!'), and just wait till you're of legal age, young man who playfully referred to me as a 'cougar'. *Grrrrrr!*

But fun sexual innuendo aside, decision-making is serious business. Time trials and skin-fold tests may get you onto the field, but your positioning and decisions will be scrutinised to uphold the highest standards. Considering my irrational, emotion-charged disposition as a female, your input has really helped ground me. Your demands from the front row to 'wipe that smirk of your face' and 'don't make any mistakes' were uplifting and confidence-boosting. I have since removed 'smirk more' and 'make more mistakes' from my life goals. Of course, when mistakes do happen, it's crucial to be held accountable. The personal anguish of making a major blunder during the match of the round was insufficient without the disgust expressed by you, talkback radio callers and certain sections of the media who remained staunchly committed to reminding us all that some people just don't belong on the field.

But like a rat in a lab experiment, I kept coming back for more ... some women just don't know when to quit. I had a deluded belief that if I could get through this, I could become the sort of umpire I really aspired to be. I worked hard to develop my 'logic' skills and assess things from a rational rather than emotional point of view. Utter confusion, then, when a call I made during a preliminary final between the Sydney Swans and Collingwood Magpies formed the basis for my next great controversy. Decisions are pretty straightforward when you're in the right position, but commentators on the live TV broadcast (who have a surprising level of influence on the public's critical-thinking ability) surmised that the most logical angle to assess the call was from a camera situated on the far wing. When will I learn?

Lucky for me, the AFL backed my call, and the following week I found myself stepping onto the hallowed turf of the MCG to officiate in the grand final. The level of interest in my appointment shocked me, with intense media attention at home and abroad. Even the *New York Times* and the BBC picked up the story. To add to the hype, Prime Minister Gillard requested access to the umpires' rooms ahead of the match. To be honest, meeting Australia's first female PM rivalled the excitement of the game itself (even though it broke the golden rule of finals football: don't change your routine). She was very relaxed and genuine, which made me comfortable in providing feedback on important issues such as wardrobe choices and hairstyles. We had a good cackle and swapped our favourite strategies for playing the gender card. 'There's one thing that matters above all else, even your values and policies,' she said, 'and that's a sharp set of kitchen knives!' I think she was referring to more than preparing high-quality home-cooked meals for her partner, Tim.

Becoming 'one of the boys' has taught me many life lessons, Thomas. How to look the other way in the change room. (To borrow a line from my favourite film, 'Sometimes in this world you see things you don't wanna see.') How to overcome feminine weaknesses such as taking forever to get ready (the bounce waits for no one) or go to the toilet without the support of a gaggle of girlfriends. I've finally grasped the concept of humour (usually lost on females). I never realised how funny farts can be, for instance (not if you do them yourself, of course – how unladylike!), never understood the comedic brilliance of tacking four simple words ('That's what she said!') onto virtually any phrase.

Admittedly, I've found coaching sessions a tad exhausting: attempting to appear assertive without being aggressive (unbecoming), open but not vulnerable (weak), communicative but not defensive (insert cat-clawing action here), self-assured but not conceited (no one likes a girl who's stuck-up). But surely that age-old conundrum of being competent *and* likeable is just a bunch of feminist baloney? I suppose the only real way of being accepted by others is learning to accept myself, as the imperfect human that I am. Failings are always front of mind, but there have been remarkable highlights, too – from the roar of the crowd on Anzac Day, to being enveloped by Port Adelaide supporters' heartfelt rendition of 'Never Tear Us Apart', to being unknowingly featured on a campaign for Sportsbet's 'big behinds' promotion.

So, Thomas, to set the record straight: nothing you've said or implied over the years has escaped my thoughtful consideration. Because being constantly reminded of your own limitations is one of the most powerful tools of encouragement.

Thanks for keepin' it real,
Chelsea

ROOKIE

Miriam Sved

My friend had come to my apartment to watch the game. I'd invited her over. I may have had motives unrelated to football. In fact I'd never had a motive related to football in my life. It was 2005 and Collingwood were doing badly.

I'd stretched my culinary and housekeeping skills – there was something I optimistically called a stir-fry (I lived alone and regularly ate breakfast cereal for dinner). I might have even bought flowers.

The game went as poorly as expected, and I was as oblivious as ever. I knew it was late in the season and that Collingwood needed a win – maybe a big win. In the last week I'd tried, in a half-arsed way, to absorb some of the particles of AFL floating everywhere in the Victorian atmosphere. Commentators were saying things like *make or break*. (Make what? Break what?) I knew what a handball was, and the difference between a goal and a behind.

At some stage that evening I left the living room, and when I came back my friend was gone. I found her outside, on my 'balcony'. We didn't really have balconies, but those of us who lived in the small apartment block maintained a shared delusion about the walkways that ran in front of the building. Pot plants were placed, in some cases deckchairs. We carefully averted our eyes and scuttled slightly when we had to walk through someone else's space.

She was sitting on the ground, back against the wall, smoking, which she'd given up. One of my neighbours – a burly man with a huge motorbike and surprisingly inaudible voice – was sitting nearby on his balcony, but we all maintained the fiction of privacy. It was awkward.

I sat down next to her and said something I hoped was appropriate about the game, how much it sucked that Collingwood were doing so badly. She didn't reply (unusual), and I realised she was crying. Or had been crying. Not in a proper, committed way; she'd clearly been trying to curb it and was trying harder now, but there was an escapee tear at the corner of her eye and she did that tough back-of-the-hand face swipe and pulled on her cigarette.

I have always liked women who fall somewhere on the masculine side of gender identity. Tomboys, women not afraid of the word *butch*. Maybe that had to do with why, since I'd moved to Melbourne a few years earlier, I'd fallen for a string of them who were more or less obsessed with footy.

There was the downy crew-cut girl who lived in Geelong; she worked at a bank and played for the local women's team. She was skinny as a rake but seemed to subsist on Mars Bars, and she would come over to my share house all bruised up, hopped up on the exercise and sugar and endearingly proud of the bruises.

There was a funny, small, intense woman – another Pies supporter. I dated her around the time of Collingwood's bad grand final defeat (any fans will know the year and won't need to be reminded of the score). She took me to meet her friends and to watch the big game at her favourite bar (in Collingwood, naturally), and over the course of the disaster got so inebriated that afterwards one of the friends had to help me peel her off a lamp post.

So I had some preparation for the tears, although no understanding of them. These men who ran around chasing a ball; mostly pretty obnoxious men, judging from the headlines (I never read beyond the headlines). The thing I couldn't grasp was: *What does it have to do with you?* There wasn't (still isn't) so much as one openly gay player in the whole league, and the only women granted some kind of peripheral belonging back then – the WAGs – were like a different species. Any overlap in the Venn diagram of us and football seemed wishful and somehow self-abasing.

I didn't say any of that. I did some stilted shoulder-patting and went back inside, left her to it. I fancied her a lot.

Two years later we were living together, and suddenly my home life revolved around the season. She dragged me to games, which wasn't completely new – I'd been dragged to games before, and been the object of two friends' recruitment drives. I figured it was part of the social contract down here: when someone clueless and uninitiated moves to Victoria you have to try and get them on-side for your team. A kind of friendly state-wide pyramid scheme. I'd briefly been a nominal Carlton supporter for one friend and a Cat for another. I'd appreciated the sheer spectacle of games at the MCG. I liked to watch the umpires, so skilled at running backwards.

The first footballer who properly caught my attention – and in this I'm sure I'm not alone – was Dale 'Daisy' Thomas. He was attention-grabbing: a gravity-defying streak of hair. He debuted in 2006 against the Crows, and by his second flying mark he pretty much ruled the world. We watched him and Mick Malthouse in interviews afterwards: I didn't expect Daisy to be so shy, so skinless and young. The thing I started to appreciate is that part of the appeal of footy, maybe of any sport, is stories. The story of an artless country boy transfigured by speed and vertical leap; of a surly old coach (flashes of charismatic warmth – you could see people following him into a cult) who likes to 'blood' his players early. Daisy weighed 68 kilos, about the same as me. He had twiggy, breakable-looking limbs, and in front of the camera he gulped and twitched like a fish. His body on the field had its own articulate self-belief. Good stories need the unexpected confluence of disparate elements: a thing we know in a place we don't expect to find it.

Daisy was my gateway narrative into footy, and he opened neatly into other, bigger stories. It was 2006, a year of surprising and, in hindsight, brilliant team-building for Collingwood. Lots of fans had gone nuts when the club used one of its highest draft picks on a lanky boy with more form in basketball than footy, but we'd seen Scott Pendlebury play and knew better: *He's a gun*. A gun, I learned, was the best thing to be. Something pointed at the opposition and fired.

It was towards the end of Nathan Buckley's playing career. He still captained the team, another narrative gem: the first time the tag *warrior* didn't seem to me like fatuous hyperbole. Face like a battering ram, issuing commands to the younger boys on the field with messianic authority (another one you'd follow into a cult). He'd left the Brisbane Bears in search of the premiership that had eluded him over a decade-long career, and now his hammies were a ticking bomb, one or maybe two seasons left in them. The crusade was irresistible.

I was also learning how other kinds of stories could be kneaded into and out of football. Collingwood was one of the founding Victorian clubs: 1892, as my new guernsey declared. It was formed in opposition to the more affluent suburban clubs and nicknamed the Purloiners by rivals. The vertical black and white stripes were meant to represent prison bars – an intimidation tactic maybe, but I preferred to see it as a middle finger to the snobby establishment. The boys who played in the early years came from one of the roughest bits of Melbourne; football was a route to respect, maybe a better life, maybe just a chance to square up to privilege on even ground. Is it naive to look for this founding spirit in the machinations of the modern professional game, with its forensic team-building and six-figure salaries? Probably, but the narrative around the modern club – at least its support base – is not so different, despite the wildly changed demographics of inner-city gentrification. You can take the toothless bogan out of Collingwood but you can't take Collingwood away from the toothless bogan. I have all my teeth, plenty of socio-economic privilege and a slightly plummy accent (although I don't know where I got that last one – I never went to private schools and my parents' families were fresh off the boat from Hungary), but who doesn't want to be one of the underdogs? Lots of people; I guess they go for Hawthorn.

Like with the trick of religious faith (which I have never mastered), as soon as I was inside the story – as soon as I *cared* – the game became hypnotic. Collingwood's was the only game I wouldn't miss every week, but I'd watch any of them. Living in the narrative immersion of footy I found, to my surprise, that I loved it all: not just the game but the whole thing, the whole shebang. It shouldn't have come as a surprise – an only child, I have always been a sucker for a sense of belonging, the comforting kinship of groupthink. Giving over to football – relaxing into the specific obsession of Collingwood and the overriding cultural intoxication of the game – turned out to come with double-admission, layers of belonging. Admission to The Club, the black and white army: a well-branded cap with *2006* in big letters next to the magpie to prove you weren't coasting on last year's membership fees. This admission gave me a sense of solidarity and fellow-feeling with a large new wedge of the world: beefy guys with cover-all tattoos smiled warmly when they saw my branding; I even became less paranoid about holding hands with my girlfriend outside the gay ghetto of the inner north. And the bigger club, the one I'd had my nose pressed up against the glass of since I moved to Melbourne: AFL. I'd just started a new job, and office chitchat became miraculously easy, even sort of enjoyable. There were a few other Pies in the office, and lots of non-Pies who enjoyed hating on us in a good-natured way. Whole significant sections of the media opened up to me; whole new *channels* – I didn't even realise how much telly I'd actively ignored until I started to care about it. Now it was all for me. I was in.

I wasn't really, but that understanding came later.

I remember 2010 as a wonderful year, a wonderful thing to be part of. The crackling excitement of the walk to the MCG with all those other people, a black and white stream up Flinders Street. There was a sense of momentum and belief building every week, until the pulse-racing pinnacle of the Big Game – both Big Games; the second, brilliant one we managed to get tickets to, and when the siren rang (Didak keeping his hands on the ball for the big moment – the players had all been playing cold potato for the last two minutes) I looked around the mosh of jubilation in the stands and made accidental eye contact with a boy in the seats in front of us – young, probably a teenager. He had tears in his eyes. Chances are, I thought, he was born into the game. He wouldn't have been alive for the last premiership win in 1990 but it would have bubbled in his family's collective memory and mythology, the undertow of his life. I knew it was sappy but I felt privileged, for a moment, to be witnessing this culmination, to have come in at the climax and happy ending of some story.

Of course there are no real endings in footy because there's always the next season. For Collingwood in 2010 there was also the next day: headlines about an *incident* involving Collingwood players after the game.

I think now that 2010 was the pinnacle of my romance with footy, the end of a heady adolescent genre and the beginning of other types of stories. That young girl in a

Richmond apartment building after the grand final. It stayed with me until Anna Krien gave it shape in *Night Games*; I was utterly persuaded by her depiction of a culture of sexual recklessness and ruthless mateship-building. Later still, Collingwood's backman Heritier Lumumba complicated the story a bit more. Fractures deep in the structure; contradictions you can't look at too closely if you want to go on cheering.

I was married by then, to the woman who'd got me into the game. Not married here, of course; we'd blown our savings and gone to San Francisco, said our vows jiggling nervously near the stately bust of Harvey Milk.

I am not an activist. Physically, constitutionally. I crumble too easily, can spend days shredding myself up over a perceived insult or something I said wrong. I internalise stupid things. I feel a combination of awe and guilt towards activists, the people who lay themselves out before the world: the tractors, the trolls, the blows that could be meant for me. Heritier Lumumba went public and eventually left the club over an incident involving homophobic graffiti in the locker room. The details were hazy and the outline didn't bear looking at.

I know people who live with the contradictions, adept at maintaining irreconcilable loves. I live with one of them.

By then I was writing fiction about football – all those intertwining stories, all that blood and pain and passion;

you can't buy that kind of narrative grist. And I did still love it; I do. I was pregnant in 2011, and during one particularly fraught finals game against the Hawks I had to leave the room and eventually the house to go for a walk and calm down – the baby was body-slamming painfully and I worried about what the waves of adrenaline were doing to her.

But I can't submerge for too long anymore; when the game ends or I push away from it I hit the surface and wonder what all the fuss was about. Perhaps my submersion therapy wasn't long enough: you have to be dunked from birth to maintain the Orwellian doublethink of true belief. The structure of the book I was writing was in place by then, but I think it turned out darker than I intended (although still lighter than the worst genres of the game). My poxy, gnarled love story.

My partner and I have a four-year-old daughter now. The week before the grand final there is Footy Day at her childcare centre: come in your colours. She knows the Collingwood theme song beginning to end and will bust it out at odd, context-free moments. She has had a junior membership since before birth; living the full-body submersion I never did. And perhaps in the year that two women's AFL teams played their televised debut at the MCG I can imagine a different sort of narrative for a woman who grows up in footy. For a woman with gay parents and my doubter's blood in her veins. I wonder how much of her story will be about the game.

'YOUR HEART WILL QUICKEN': THE DEATH AND BIRTH OF A FAN

Tony Birch

When the Fitzroy Football Club was put to the economic-rationalist sword at the end of the 1996 AFL season, I came to miss many things that had defined my life for more than thirty-five years. What I yearned for most in the immediate years following the death of my club were the Saturday winter afternoons I had enjoyed full of hope and the dreams I wove out of deluded optimism. Although those days and dreams so often ended in a humiliating loss, I was willing to dream again – and again.

Whenever I want to replenish my attachment to Fitzroy I head for the old Brunswick Street oval and allow its spirit to draw me in. It is a place I sometimes feel an urgent need to return to, particularly when I have been thrown by something in my life that may have nothing to do with football. The ground is a place where I reclaim my past and occasionally puzzle over who I am now.

Recently, I again walked from my home in nearby Carlton to the oval. It was a bitter Saturday morning. It never felt this cold when I was kid, I convinced myself as I buttoned my coat against the sharp breeze. I had never been deterred by bad weather in the early 1960s, when the ground was wrapped in a concrete wall and I was convinced that the players waited on the other side of the wall for me to come and watch them play.

As I do each time I return, I walked a lap of the oval that morning. I began by passing what remains of the northern entrance, with the remnants of its ticketing booths in place. It is the spot where I would line up of a Saturday afternoon to get into the ground, where I would become anxious, thinking I might miss the first bounce. I casually circled the oval remembering a freakish goal kicked from the half-forward flank, or a spectacular mark taken on the wing, more often by an opposition player. I reconfigured the outer terraces where I played kick-to-kick with my older brother long after the game was over and our father finished off a beer with his mates.

After my lap of honouring them, I walked up the creaking wooden steps of the old grandstand and sat on one of the wooden benches, gazing across to a city skyline of high-rise towers that did not exist in the 1960s. Looking down at the oval I was reminded of the poem 'Old Fitzroy' by Tom Petsinis, and in particular its poignant ending:

> The oval's size has remained unchanged
> For players recalled from suspension in the past.
> You'll catch the echo of your own applause,
> Your heart will quicken on the wing.

And don't the poets know the truth? My heart did quicken as I experienced an emotional vibration. It doesn't surprise me that while I have erased many of the losses I witnessed at the ground, each time I visit I can look across the grass and easily conjure the 'field of dreams' of pre-season training, when hope was everything, yet to be buried in the mud of winter.

My father always sat in the grandstand during pre-season training, to get a better look at a new kid down from the bush, or a northern suburban club with the unlikely name of Preston Swimmers. The light was always sweeter on those afternoons, and the casual optimism of the small crowd could lull a small boy to sleep.

Before leaving the grandstand I looked to the area behind the Brunswick Street goals, to where I stood with my family, friends, urgers and other hangers-on during the season. We were our own crowd, and we clung together over the years as we moved from Brunswick Street to Princes Park, then the Junction Oval, where we played our best football, then briefly to Victoria Park, then back to Princes Park, before being banished to the Western Oval, where we became a ragged band of refugees, worn down and worn out by neglect.

Filled with the sadness of this thought I sometimes leave the Brunswick Street ground chilled, with a sense of grief enveloping me.

As a kid my maroon and navy football jumper warmed me, with the number 7 on the back. The maroon was of such a deep hue that on a murky day it was difficult to distinguish it from the navy. I wore the number 7 in honour of Wally Clark, our 'first rover' during the late 1950s and early '60s. Wally was built like a butcher's apprentice and played 105 games for the club. I have never admitted this publicly, out of loyalty to Wally, but I was always envious that I did not wear the number 2 jumper, sported by my older brother. It was the young Kevin Murray's number. He wore it winning seven Best and Fairest awards before heading across the country to Perth in 1965. He returned to the club for the 1967 season, to a hero's homecoming and the coveted number 1 jumper. Prior to 1967 the club had collected three of the previous four seasons' wooden spoons and had won only six games. There should have been little reason for such optimism the following season.

The first practice game of the 1967 season was held at an unfenced suburban oval in East Brunswick. I caught the tram with my father and older brother. All we could talk about was Murray's return to the club – Murray the Messiah. My father went over great Kevin Murray moments of the past, clenched his fist and made the unambiguous statement, 'He is Fitzroy.' Rather than take the coming season 'one week at a time', as all football fans are drilled to do, my father was talking finals by the time we got off the tram.

The picturesque ground had its changing rooms in the bowels of a small grandstand. In those days you could get into the rooms before the game, and with some embarrassment, approach a genuine leaguer footballer, who would often be naked except for his jockstrap, and ask for his autograph.

I have never forgotten seeing Murray that day, wearing a sleeveless generic practice jumper and the jockstrap as he talked to a sports reporter wearing a suit and tie. The reporter was furiously taking notes, hanging on every word Murray spoke. My brother, who was drenched in sweat, as he had decided to wear his Fitzroy jumper to the ground on a hot late-summer day, pointed in the direction of Murray and whispered, 'Look, it's him.' I could not take my eyes off his oiled and tattooed arms. His muscular shoulders resembled knots of steel to a ten-year-old boy.

We left the ground full of uncharacteristic bravado. For not only had the warrior himself returned from the Wild West, a seventeen-year-old made his debut on the same patch of grass. The boy could play on both sides of his body and suffered leather poisoning as he racked up possession after possession that the stats men of old, armed with nothing more than lead in their pencils and sharp eyes, could hardly keep pace with. The kid's name was John Murphy, and he would go on to captain the club and win five Best and Fairest awards.

Unfortunately, reality set in within weeks of the season commencing. While we did not finish on the bottom of the ladder in 1967, we were only one spot above twelfth, and won just four games. By the time Fitzroy eventually did get to play finals football, twelve years later, in 1979, Murray had been retired for five years, and Murphy had moved to another club.

I should have realised it that day, back in 1967, that we were not about to play finals football. Even though I was just ten years old, I knew this in my head even though my heart continued to deceive me. But had my head ruled my understanding of football, my life as a fan would have resembled something like common sense. Had I thought that way, I would not have gone to the football each week and happily stood in the rain watching a team that battled to win just a few games a season for the entire decade of the 1960s, most of the 1970s, about half of the '80s and all of the 1990s, until the end came. There is nothing more vital to the longevity of a dedicated supporter of a struggling club than an acute ability to defy logic. It is what keeps us going.

For many years I trudged away from suburban football grounds after yet another Fitzroy defeat. In the early days it was back up Brunswick Street to our narrow terrace, and the solace of a warm fire. On occasion it was the humiliating walk to a suburban railway station, and a miserable and silent train ride home after being taunted by cruel opposition supporters.

Or it was the long walk home from the MCG, through the Fitzroy Gardens, bottomed out with depression by the time I hit the model Tudor Village. It was on those walks that hope and madness were reborn out of despair. Despite having just been beaten by ten goals or more my older brother would be the one to break our glum silence, reminding me that we had been unlucky. 'I mean really unlucky,' he would insist, like he believed it.

'If the wind hadn't died in the last quarter,' he would observe, and if the ball had not bounced that way, and if they had not been better than us – maybe, just maybe, we would have got up and won. He would pull the football record out of his pocket and run down the list of players, announcing who would be back from injury the following week. He would then laud the kid from the thirds who had just kicked four in his first game in the seconds; the kid who was ready for the seniors.

By the time we reached the other side of the park, and

we'd reminded ourselves that we had the home ground advantage the following week, and even though we were playing last year's premiers who had thrashed us in the first round, we knew – without doubt – that we were a chance, a real chance. This was all it took to encourage us to huddle around the radio the following Thursday night, listening to the teams being read out, and plan the coming weekend around just the one activity – football.

Just as my memory of conversations full of hope, or a practice game at an obscure suburban oval 1967 remain lucid, there are moments I would prefer to forget, such as sitting in the MCG's Ponsford Stand for Fitzroy's final Melbourne game, against the Richmond Football Club in 1996. As many did that day, I sat in the stand after the game and cried. As devastated as I was, I did not want to leave the ground that day, and sat long after the game was over. I knew that once I turned my back and walked away as a Fitzroy supporter for the final time there would be nothing to come back to.

I remember little about that game itself, except that we were thrashed, as we had been thrashed for most of that season. Nor do I have any memory of who played that day. But I do remember walking through the Fitzroy Gardens and finding nothing to lift my spirits when I reached the other side. I was emptied of every emotion but grief. There was nothing to hope for, nothing to look forward to, or worry over for next week. There would be no next season for me. Granted, we had a final game to play the following week, against Fremantle in Perth. It might just as well have been played on another planet. I didn't bother watching the game on television as I regarded it as the AFL's ultimate insult to the club. It was a death without the funeral.

On the day that the misnomer referred to as a 'merger' with the Brisbane Bears Football Club was announced, 4 July 1996, my grandmother died. For a week prior to that day I had sat in a St Vincent's Hospital window overlooking the landscapes of both our lives; the houses we'd lived in and the streets we'd walked together. That night I left the hospital with my family. We were going back to my mother's house, in Collingwood, for a cup of tea and a good cry. I got in my car, turned on the radio and heard the news that remnants of our club would be heading north to join Brisbane.

My older sister, who loved the Fitzroy Football Club as deeply as any of us, let out a sad laugh, before swearing angrily. 'Fuck me,' she screamed, 'no wonder Nan dropped dead. She must have known this shit was about to hit the fan.'

At my mother's request we drove down Brunswick Street towards the old ground. I passed the oval, did a U-turn and drove by a second time. I could hear my mother whispering. I did not have to ask her what she was doing. It might have been a whole rosary she was reciting, or perhaps just one Hail Mary. I could not be sure. But I did know that she was praying for the dead.

I learned a lot from the death of my club. Let me pass on my wisdom, born out of sorrow and heartbreak. Firstly, there is a situation far worse than following a football club that cannot win a game. And that is to have no club at all. When you do not have a club you are less than a week-to-week proposition. You are nothing. Secondly, there is no joy in becoming a neutral and objective football follower. This is the tragedy that awaits the clubless. You become a boring know-it-all, capable of little but sitting in front of the TV, or in the stands at a game, explaining the rules and the decision-making process to the passionate, irrational and perhaps even psychotic fan. Nobody wants you.

Objectivity and logic became my sad existence after 1996, as I had no will to follow the sun-drenched Lions. I held no animosity towards the Brisbane Bears. Other AFL clubs were as eager to swallow the Roys. It was simply not possible for me to follow an interstate-based club. It made no sense to someone who had experienced the game as so territorial and parochial, even if territory and local identity had become a state of mind for most Melbourne-based supporters by the 1990s, rather than the geographic realities of the past.

Regardless, I made a conscious decision to watch early season Brisbane Lions games in 1997, deciding, as always, that I would let emotion rule over my head. If my heart led me north, then I was willing to go, perhaps reluctantly. I watched those games – closely. And nothing happened. My heart rate did not increase a single beat. I felt no more or less connection to the club than I did for any other that I occasionally watched on TV. By halfway through the season I was both disappointed and relieved that the Brisbane Lions would not be my club. I no longer had a club, but I still had Fitzroy, intact and whole, but unfortunately extinct. Even when Brisbane won their three successive flags I was not lured. I watched a fair bit of them on television and was happy to see them win. They were a champion team, one of the best I have seen. But they were not my team.

I spent years in the wilderness watching football on television. I had toyed with the possibility of following another Melbourne club. I went to a few Richmond games but quickly realised one had to carry the Richmond DNA from birth to follow the club. The Tigers do not adopt, unless you're a garbo or a meatworker. I even thought about Collingwood, on the selfish grounds of survival alone; my rationale being that a club as powerful as Collingwood could never go out of business. Mercifully, the thought didn't last long, as I realised that attempting a switch from Fitzroy to Collingwood was far too audacious a proposition, and beyond my station in football life.

And then there was Footscray, a club I'd always had a soft spot for, due to reasons other than the way they played the game. I had always liked their jumper, and began to have fantasies about my children getting around in Doggies guernseys, not that they'd been consulted. I also fondly remembered being at a Fitzroy–Footscray game as a kid and being hit in the face and knocked off my feet by a Ted Whitten stab kick. But I could not follow the Dogs in good faith as I still felt the shame of the pathetic attempt by some in the Fitzroy (and Footscray) administration to attempt a merger in 1989. I was also troubled by the thought that they were a little too much like Fitzroy; everyone liked them – they were relatively harmless – but not enough people barracked for them. Therefore they were also a threatened species.

By 2002 I could accept my self-imposed exile no longer. When I saw other delirious supporters celebrating at a game, or being carried away in straightjackets after a one-point loss, I became insanely, even homicidally jealous. So at the beginning of the 2003 season I became a Carlton supporter, a club chosen with no more logic than I had been born in Carlton, and that after 1996 my mother had gone back to following the club she had grown up supporting. (When she married my father her dowry had consisted of a set of linen doilies and a pledge to switch to Fitzroy).

I was also attracted to the Carlton jumper and club song, both of which bleed a rich history. I walked into Princes Park for the first game of that 2003 season with a sense of unreality, but to my surprise I walked out at the end of the game, which Carlton lost, with an immediate and unexplainable sense of attachment. Maybe it helped that I had been away from the game for six years. Some of the Carlton players I had once hated when they were so swaggeringly successful had retired, while their immediate past president, whose brand of politics or football administration I did not share, had resigned. And while the Carlton Football Club is to some a silvertail outfit, the supporters I rubbed shoulders with that day at the Heatley end of the ground were the voices from the migrant and working class suburbs of the north – Brunswick, Coburg and points beyond.

I decided from that day to commit to the club, totally. I go to most home games and watch the interstate trips on TV. I quickly discovered my own 'kids', the young recruits who I spotted something special in, just as my dad had done watching practice games in the 1960s. My younger daughters went immediately crazy for the club, while my two older daughters, who had grown up also following Fitzroy, came in from the cold. So I am a Carlton supporter. They are loved by many, and hated by more; such is the way of great clubs that rarely become a supporter's second team. They are not Fitzroy, but nor are they a substitute. They are my club on earth, while 'as it is in heaven' remains Fitzroy, the team I visit occasionally on my walks at the Brunswick Street Oval, where in my heart I compile lists, such as the five greatest Fitzroy players of the my era – which for the record are Kevin Murray, John Murphy, Paul Roos, Bernie Quinlan and, the best of the best, Gary Wilson – all courage, all class, and forever Fitzroy.

MARNGROOK, THE WOMEN OF *MARNGROOK* AND THE 'R' WORD

Leila Gurruwiwi

Who would've thought that a very shy young girl, who started life in one of Australia's most remote (and some people would argue most disadvantaged, but I would say differently) Indigenous communities, would now be working on an extremely successful Indigenous AFL football show and living in the spiritual home of AFL – Melbourne?

Well, that's me: Lorell Rirryalpi Mindhili Gurruwiwi. But you can call me Leila.

I lived in the tiny island community of Galiwinku on Elcho Island (don't worry! I don't expect you to know where that is!) with my biological family until I was eighteen months old. My parents thought I would have more opportunities elsewhere, so I left them and three older brothers – and the little sister who was on the way – in the Northern Territory and moved with an extended family member to Bendigo, Victoria.

Footy kind of runs in my blood. When my dad was alive, he was a very good sportsman and played footy. Most of my brothers, nephews, uncles and cousins have played footy at one point or another and, like in most remote communities in the NT, footy is a big part of the Galiwinku community in general. Even now they have a women's league there.

I have lots of fond memories of Bendigo, mainly of my closest friend, Bridgette Griffin (now Scilini), and her family, who are all one-eyed Carlton supporters, and my aunty Louise Moore and her family, who are crazy about footy too. Bridgette wore badges of her favourite Carlton players on the underside of her wedding dress as her 'something blue', and when I ring Aunty Lou during the footy season I know not to expect her to pick up the phone if her Maggies are playing!

In 2005 I moved to Melbourne, and finished Year 12 a year later; a highlight was my mum coming down to see me graduate. And in 2007, at the age of nineteen, I found myself a new family: the *Marngrook Footy Show* family.

I believe that sometimes you are just in the right place at the right time for doors to open in your life. I was definitely in the right place in 2007 when *Marngrook*, which until that point was a radio show commissioned by the new National Indigenous television station (NITV), became a national Indigenous footy show. Creator Grant Hansen noticed that there was no platform for Indigenous players to be seen or heard within mainstream AFL radio and TV shows, so when *Marngrook* had the chance to become a national television show with the help and support of NITV, Grant saw his dream coming to fruition. And he wanted to take me along for the ride.

I wasn't sure if I would be able to do it, having just finished high school six months earlier. I had no direction or career I wanted to follow; I had no media experience and didn't really have a lot of self-confidence at the time. But, fortunately, Grant had enough confidence in me for the both of us, and pushed me into the deep end, and for that I am very thankful. Without him, I would not be doing all the wonderful things that I do now – including writing this piece about my experiences in AFL!

I recently watched our very first episode of *The Marngrook Footy Show*, which aired back in 2007. Watching the panel made up of Grant Hansen, Gilbert McAdam, Ronnie Burns, Alan Thorpe, Derek Kickett, Emily Fien and, of course, myself, with our very first special guest, Nathan Lovett-Murray, I must admit there was more than a little bit of cringing on my behalf. But it also made me realise how far we have come since then. From a tiny studio at RMIT and a bunch of nervous people who didn't know what they'd got themselves into (the only person with any TV experience at that time was Grant), to over 250 episodes, a series of Logies nominations, booked-out audiences months in advance, and the whole *Marngrook* team looking and feeling very comfortable in front of TV cameras.

AFL is a male-dominated sport and that goes for the AFL media space too. I work with more than my fair share of men every Thursday night on the *Marngrook Footy Show* (someone has to keep them all in line!) but never once has my value as a part of the *Marngrook* crew ever been questioned or undermined. Shelley Ware and I have always been seen as an integral part of the show's success. I think it is very important to have female voices talking about footy and all the issues that surround it, because we love the game just as much as our male counterparts. Women have always been a big part of the fabric of AFL, and it is great to see more and more women stepping into this space.

I have a few favourite moments that made me realise the impact I've made. The first was when my niece was caught by her mum (my sister-in-law) putting on make-up in her bedroom. When she was queried about it she told her mum that she 'wanted to be like Aunty Leila!' The second time was when my mum was in another remote community, walking to the local take-away, when two girls walked past her and one said to the other, 'See that lady over there? That's Leila Gurruwiwi's mum!'

Even though she doesn't tell me much, I know my mum is very proud of me. Every single staff member at her school – she's a teacher at Shepherdsen College on Elcho Island – tells me how much she talks about me; what I'm wearing on the show, who I'm interviewing, what my hair looks like. I feel the pride my family has for me when I go home to Galiwinku.

Funnily enough, even though there are so many men on *Marngrook*, some of the strongest bonds I have made are with the women I have had the chance to meet and work with. Bev, our gorgeous wardrobe lady who I have fun with choosing clothes to wear on set; Sue and Mon, our great make-up ladies who, even when we're not looking our best, make sure we're ready for the camera; Danni, our amazing director's assistant and production manager who always comes into the make-up room before the show to chat; and all the wonderful, strong Indigenous women who have been beside me since the show started: Emily Fien, Kylie Farmer, Sandy Greenwood and Shelley Ware. In 2015, more than ever, I needed their strength. In mid June, my fiancé Zach and I lost our baby (which would have been our first together) at sixteen weeks. It was heartbreaking for both of us but I drew a lot of strength from being with these women who knew me well and understood what I was going through.

Sometimes, when such a big loss happens, people don't know how to act or what to say. I found this true both at work and in my life outside of work, but being with my *Marngrook* family helped me a lot; it made me feel normal, which was very important to me at the time.

Gilly, a huge favourite on *Marngrook*, isn't a fella of too many words – off the panel, anyway. But the week I was back on the show he gave me a gorgeous gift that made me realise how much everyone was thinking of me when we lost our bub. It was a beautiful pink pouch containing the oddest and most random things, with a little note explaining the gifts: 'A coin so that you are always rich, a candle so that you are always in the light, a marble so you never lose yours, a rubber band so you can bounce back, a piece of string to keep things together and a kiss to remind you that someone cares about you.'

I get emotional just writing it, but that gift solidified how important my *Marngrook* family was to me.

Besides going to Etihad Stadium and being able to watch the Western Bulldogs play, my favourite time in the AFL calendar is Indigenous Round. These days I no longer get nervous before shows, except before our Indigenous Round special. I'm not quite sure why, but every single year it's the same. The young men from the Footy Means Business Program fill up all the seats in our audience. We get to showcase an amazing Indigenous artist at the end of our show, and Shelley and I do our best to source Indigenous designers so we can wear their jewellery and clothes on air. We also do what we always do, and yet still I get nervous. Maybe it's because I understand that this is the week we are showcasing ourselves, our culture, and our heritage to the wider community. It means a lot to know that the AFL wants to celebrate the wonderful contribution the Indigenous community makes to the game and to have a match every year is very special to all of us. But, sadly, this year's Indigenous Round created what would later become a dark cloud over the footy season.

As everyone knows, 2015 had been a crazy year. It felt like it was nearly consumed by the 'booing saga' surrounding Adam Goodes. I have been subjected to and witnessed racism – both blatantly and subtly – in the wider community and within the AFL scene, and until you have been somewhere where you are seen as different because of the colour of your skin, you can't truly understand how it feels. How it hits at the core of your being, that someone thinks it's okay to mock you and your ancestral lineage. The incident polarised many people, and changed their perception of whether there is still racism in this country. I know for a fact there still is racism in this country, and there's still a lot of work that needs to be done. But whether you believe that the booing was racist or not, as soon as someone lets you know that it is affecting their wellbeing, it should stop. And it did, eventually. People needed to realise that this was affecting someone's mental and spiritual health. While watching the Retiring Legends Lap of Honour around the

MCG at the grand final in 2015, it was very sad to see one empty seat. But I understand why Adam chose not to be a part of it, and I fully support his decision. Adam is an amazing footballer, a great man and role model to all Indigenous people. He has had enormous success, on the field and off. I wish him nothing but the best in all he does after AFL.

I don't know what the future holds for *The Marngrook Footy Show* or for myself, but with all the amazing people I have met and worked with, all the wonderful opportunities that have opened up for me because of my work on *Marngrook* – including emceeing events, doing cultural awareness talks in schools, acting both on television and on stage, being able to visit Indigenous communities I've never been to before, and mentoring young Indigenous girls – I would not trade my life for anything. I am truly grateful for all that I have done and have experienced. I hope that I have inspired some young Indigenous girls out there to believe in themselves and, who knows? We might see more young Indigenous girls follow their dreams into the AFL arena – and maybe even a few more AFL TV presenters like myself!

THE PURPLE BOMBER

Jason Tuazon-McCheyne as told to Jacqueline Tomlins

I knew I was gay when I was five years old. I didn't use that word, of course, or understand exactly what it meant, but I knew I was different. I loved Buck Rogers and Luke Skywalker and not in the way other boys did; I was drawn to them. There was definitely a sense of attraction and I think, in some childlike way, I was *in love* with them.

At twelve I went on my first camp and the boys were obsessed with kissing the girls. I couldn't have been less interested and actually found the whole idea repugnant. I remember one of the boys saying, 'Jase, let's go kiss the girls!' and I ran in the opposite direction. Literally.

I didn't tell anyone how I felt. What would I have said? How would I have explained it? I didn't really understand it myself. I never felt there was anything wrong with me, but I also knew – instinctively – that other people would think there was. I learnt very early that I shouldn't talk about my feelings for boys, but more than that, I learnt that I should be especially careful to hide those feelings. Somehow, even then, I sensed danger.

I fell in love with football when I was very young too. My mum's partner barracked for Essendon and I would get kitted out in footy shorts and a black and red jumper and we'd head off to Windy Hill. I remember running through the legs of all these huge grown-ups and gathering peanuts as they fell to the ground. And when there were no more peanuts I'd collect the ring pulls from soft drink cans and make them into daisy chains. I couldn't actually see much of the footy, because I was too small, but eventually someone thought to bring a stool and I got my first proper look at the game.

Even then, at that early age, I knew that liking boys and liking footy didn't go together. Somehow that message was conveyed to me very clearly, and it would be decades before I would start to reconcile these two fundamental parts of my life.

At thirteen I really started to get into the game. I remember dressing from head to toe in my Essendon gear and watching the '83 grand final from the couch in my lounge room. We kicked one goal in the first quarter then lost by 83 points. I was absolutely crushed. After that I began going to games every week. When Hawthorn beat us by eight points in the '84 second semifinal I was gutted. And when we won the grand final two weeks later I burst into tears. It's a bit embarrassing really, but that's how it was.

I started working at the footy on the weekends when I was fifteen. I sold souvenirs in one of those little caravans outside the ground. On grand final day that year my boss got me into the game for free and I stayed until the cup presentation. I watched from the standing area; the whole thing was completely electrifying – and my boss paid me for the day too! After that I was totally hooked. I'd travel all over Melbourne to get to matches – sometimes on two trains and a bus and in the pouring rain. I've been doing that most of life – though not the bus and train part – and recently I got my thirty-year membership card.

When I was sixteen something happened that haunted me for the next twenty-five years. I was at home one Saturday afternoon watching a TV interview with Simon Madden, a legend of the club. I can't recall the exact words he used, but he said that the Essendon Football Club was no place for people who were gay. I remember feeling absolutely shattered. I had this intense passion for this football club, but I was also gay and here I was being told quite explicitly that those two things were incompatible. My fundamental sense of self – who I was – and the thing I loved most in the world – Essendon Football Club – were irreconcilable and that broke my heart. Recently I had coffee with Simon and told him that story. He didn't remember saying it, but he did say he'd evolved, moved on, and that wasn't what he thought now.

Despite all that I still followed the game obsessively. I spent a number of years in the United States in the early '90s and a friend of mine would cut out newspaper articles and mail them to me. At the beginning of the year he would fax me the fixtures and I'd call my mum after the match for the result – and those phone calls were extortionately expensive back then. I flew home twice for matches, and in '93 when I couldn't get home I drove for six hours through Missouri to Nebraska to get to a TV that was showing the grand final at two o'clock in the morning. And it was oh so worth it because we beat Carlton and won the flag.

In '98 I met my now husband, Adrian, who wasn't into footy as much as I was – that wouldn't be hard, I know – but he started coming to games with me. The following season we lost the preliminary final by one point even though we were the best team that year. It was one of the most tragic days of my life. I was depressed for weeks and almost needed therapy.

I'd met Adrian through a dating website, and after our initial phone call we'd talked three or four times. We'd decided to meet for dinner at Blue Train in Southgate, but as there were no photos on gay.com I told him I'd be wearing an Essendon scarf, and that's how he recognised me.

We had a great dinner and a really good chat and I

thought he was lovely. I called him the following morning and we met again the next day and we've been together ever since – eighteen years now. Meeting Adrian was a catalyst for my coming out, and also for starting to challenge the homophobia I saw in the game I loved. How that happened wasn't planned; it came right out of the blue and surprised even me.

Adrian and I were sitting in our reserved seats at Etihad Stadium watching the game when a guy behind us started shouting. He was abusing the umpires and the opposition players and was yelling, 'You fucking poofters!' 'You bloody faggots!' Moments later a teenage girl next to him – his daughter – started shouting the same stuff. We were trying to watch the game while listening to this horrible homophobic abuse in loud stereo behind us.

I turned to Adrian and said, 'I can't listen to this. I just can't.' I'm not a confrontational or antagonistic person, but I just couldn't let it go. My heart was pounding and I was really shaky, but I turned around and caught the guy's eye. 'Look,' I said quite calmly. 'I'm gay and this is my husband. Can you please not use the words "poofter" and "faggot"? They're really offensive. Can you use some other language?' I turned back around to Adrian, scared shitless of what would happen next. But nothing did. I reckon the guy was pretty shocked, but he didn't say a word for the rest of the game.

And because we had reserved seats, he was there when we rocked up the following week. But he still didn't say anything. Eventually we moved to a different part of the stadium which, I have to admit, was a relief. But I never regretted saying what I did and I think that moment set me on a direct path to setting up the Purple Bombers. Adrian and I have a son now, Ruben, and I want to be able to take him to the footy and for us to feel safe as a family; I don't want Ruben to hear that kind of language.

About four years ago Adrian and I decided to sponsor a player and we picked Brendon Goddard the day he signed up. As part of that sponsorship arrangement we were invited to three or four events throughout the year and had the opportunity to develop a closer relationship with the club. We went along to the preseason Chairman's Dinner and sat on a table with Brendon, his fellow player Joe Daniher and four other supporters.

Part way through the dinner I began to suspect that two of the other people at our table were a gay couple as well. That meant half the people around that table were gay, but at no point during the evening did any of us reveal that; effectively we were all sitting there completely closeted. On the way home I remember thinking, *I can't do this anymore. Here I am giving money to the club. I'm at a corporate event having dinner with the players and I am afraid to be myself. It's ridiculous.*

Coincidently around that time I met Marc Bertieri, who was working for Essendon in the social media area. I shared my concerns with him and asked how he thought the club would respond if I approached them about tackling homophobia. He went back to the club and spoke to some key people and the response was very positive.

I decided to take the next step and arranged a meeting with Ryan Mckee, the marketing manager. I told him that Essendon had an opportunity to take the lead on tackling homophobia both within the club and the AFL more broadly. I proposed the idea of an LGBTI supporters' club and a pride game the following season. He was really receptive to both.

What happened next was awesome. The club invited me to participate in a press conference with Brendon before the Essendon versus Sydney game. After feeling so marginalised for so many years, here I was standing next to one of the leading players, talking to the media about establishing the Purple Bombers. The following day Adrian, Ruben and I flew up to Sydney for the game and the club filmed us for *Bomber TV.* The whole thing was a complete buzz.

We put the call out for supporters interested in being part of the Purple Bombers and the club set up a webpage. They copped some flack on social media with fans threatening to tear up their membership if they went ahead. One person posted, 'Why do they need their own group?'

Brendon responded by saying, '*They* don't need their own group. *We* need it.' I loved that.

Around 150 people replied to our call and we set up a committee with an equal number of lesbians and gay men. We established three aims: to have a pride game at AFL level; to help establish similar groups at other clubs (Collingwood's Pink Magpies were the first and now there are five in total); and to make the AFL a safer place for LGBTI fans and players. We launched the Purple Bombers at a fabulous event in the city sponsored by Herbert Smith Freehills. I talked about my journey; the CEO, Xavier Campbell, outlined the club's 'Respect' campaign, and Brendon publically outed his niece.

Just recently we had our first pride event, which was hosted by the club at Etihad Stadium before the game. It was attended by over 150 people and there was entertainment, food and drink and some great speakers: Rowena Allen, Victoria's first Gender and Sexuality Commissioner, and a champion of the game, 91-year-old Jack Jones. I was so proud that EFC had taken this first bold step. They now have a strategic plan for tackling homophobia and are aiming to be the most inclusive club in the AFL.

The next sponsors' event was very different for me. At the mid-season ball, Brendon, who was hosting, welcomed the Purple Bombers and, for the first, time I felt acknowledged. I even got up and danced – not that I'm a very good dancer, in fact I'm a hopeless dancer – but I felt safe to be on the dance floor with Adrian and that was a huge shift. I wasn't trying to make a statement; it was just about being visible. Nobody batted an eyelid, but I felt that if anyone had reacted negatively a number of people in that room would have defended us. For me, that was hugely important and a very significant turning point.

Recently, I was doing a segment on Joy 94.9 FM with entertainer Dolly Diamond and transgender advocate Michelle Sheppard. Michelle was explaining that now she has transitioned she no longer goes to her children's school; she doesn't want her kids to have to deal with negative fall-out because of her. She was crying when she said it and I thought it was one of the saddest things I'd heard anyone say for a long time. She also said that she wanted to go to the footy, but since transitioning she was too afraid.

After the show I offered to go with her to a game and a few weeks later we went to see the Bulldogs play West Coast. I waited outside the ground to meet her and, I have to admit, I was pretty nervous myself. We ended up having a great day; chatting a lot and just enjoying each other's company. And, coincidently, we sat very close to the spot where I had first challenged that supporter about his homophobic language. Since then, Michelle has been to four Essendon games and has swapped her Bulldogs' jumper for a red and black one. And she feels safe.

I also feel safer now. I feel that people will at least be held accountable for homophobic comments and behaviour, and that's different from before. I'm really proud of what we've achieved so far and there's going to be a full pride game this season. Can you imagine, the message that would be sent to all the LGBTI players and supporters, especially all the young kids out there, by a ground covered in rainbow flags?

For most of the year my head is full of footy – trading, drafting, fixtures, wins and defeats – it never goes away. It's my time out, my mental focus, my relaxation. It's something I share every week with my husband and son. But I'm also gay and, as an advocate, that occupies a lot of headspace too. I feel like, finally, there is a chance for these two fundamental parts of myself to come together.

I know there are still many people within football who do not see this issue as important and who have no interest in challenging homophobia or furthering the cause of equality. It raises the question: 'Is football just about winning premierships or can it play a role in bringing about social change?' I think it's about both. Football is such a big part of many people's lives – and of the Australian culture – and I believe it has the potential to create enormous change; it can lead that change. I know it can be confronting for people, but change is happening everywhere and we need to embrace it and celebrate it wherever we can. Even in football. Especially in football.

I think back to when I was a kid and I first fell in love with the game, and then heard that terrible message that I wasn't welcome at my club. For most of my life I've felt on the outer. I haven't felt included. I haven't felt I could be myself. For me, on a personal level, that's definitely changed, but our challenge now is to change it for everyone. I want every LGBTI person in the crowd, at any game, to feel safe, to feel included, and to know they belong.

FOOTY DREAMS IN STRUGGLETOWN

Alice Pung & Nick Cadle

Nick

1.

When I was eleven or twelve I went to Windy Hill for a football clinic. My parents had bought me a junior membership, and I joined hundreds of other little Essendon fans for a day of running about doing football drills with the hopes of impressing Kevin Sheedy enough for him to offer us a contract.

This was my one opportunity to see the players whom I could otherwise only see in highlights on the news. I saw Michael Long and Dean Rioli, players whose on-field elegance matched their off-field demeanour. It was amazing. But there was one player who popped my eyes right out of their sockets. Where the other players just seemed like better versions of the players running around my local oval on Saturdays, this guy was different. This guy looked like he could pick up Michael Long and Dean Rioli and carry them both around the oval. His bicep was the size of my head. I had never heard of this guy because he had never played a game, but he was, in fact, on the Essendon list. He was a football player, but not like any other football player I had seen before. His name was Dwayne Armstrong.

Dwayne Armstrong was the first guinea pig in Kevin Sheedy's experiment of bringing super athletes from overseas to play football. This was during the late 1990s, and players were required to run faster, jump higher and be stronger, and to be able to do all of these things for longer than ever before. Australian athletic potential is a speck on the mountain of global athletic potential. The logical conclusion was that it was easier to find someone on the mountain than it was to look in the speck. It was easier to take the best athletes and just teach them how to play football. That's how an NFL player came to Melbourne.

It was not hard to see why Dwayne Armstrong was chosen. He was carved from stone. He had the confidence of someone who knows who he is and how much better he is than you. The trouble was, he couldn't play Aussie Rules. The skills are so alien to anything else in any other sport; it's like learning a foreign language. You can have perfect pronunciation and have the vocabulary of a university professor, but if you are not practising it inside a family or community that speaks it, there is just something missing.

Dwayne Armstrong is now no more than a stub on Wikipedia. But the search for physiologically out-of-this-world athletes continues. There are now three American-born players on AFL lists: Eric Wallace (Collingwood), Jason Holmes (St Kilda) and Mason Cox (North Melbourne). We met both Eric and Jason, both college graduates, when they first arrived in Melbourne. The US Embassy was holding a welcome. Jason mentioned that he was surprised by the rigor of training in AFL, how alcohol was prohibited during the season, and how what they ate was monitored. But the thing that baffled the Americans the most was how the game is played: thirty-six players swarm over the field and collide with each other under some form of loosely organised chaos.

2.

There is an Aboriginal language known as Guugu Yimithirr, spoken by people in far-north Queensland. 'Guugu' means 'language' and 'yimi-thirr' means 'this way', so the people who speak Guugu Yimithirr are people who speak 'this kind of language' or 'speak this way'. As Guy Deutscher explains in his wonderful book *Through the Language Glass*, the distinctive feature of this language is how it is used to describe space, or more accurately, the speaker's location and relationship with space.

Most languages use an egocentric system of spatial language: the individual is at the centre of everything.

When describing direction to the library, you might say, 'turn left at the next lights, then turn right when you pass the shops.' However, the Guugu Yimithirr language is geographically based – speakers of this language do not use words for 'left' and 'right' to describe directions, nor do they use 'behind' or 'in front of' to describe their position in relation to other objects. The individual is an inseparable part of the landscape. To orient themselves and provide direction, they only use the four cardinal directions: north, south, east and west. If a Westerner were walking through the bush with a friend and a snake slithered across the track in front of them, they would say, 'Watch out for that snake in front of you.' A Guugu Yimithirr speaker, on the other hand, would say, 'Watch out for that snake to the north of your foot.' The really weird part is that this all seems innate and intuitive. Deautscher goes on to explain how the linguist Stephen Levinson studied the Guugu Yimithirr in the 1980s:

> He took Guugu Yimithirr speakers on various trips to unfamiliar places, both walking and driving, and then tested their orientation. In their region, it is rarely possible to travel in a straight line, since the route often has to go around bogs, mangrove swamps, rivers, mountains, sand dunes, forests, and, if on foot, snake-infested grassland. But even so, and even when they were taken to dense forests with no visibility, even

> inside caves, they always, without any hesitation, could point accurately to the cardinal directions. They don't do any conscious computations: they don't look at the sun and pause for a moment of calculation before saying 'the ant is north of your foot.' They seem to have perfect pitch for directions. They simply feel where north, south, west and east are, just as people with perfect pitch hear what each note is without having to calculate intervals.[1]

Language changes the perception of reality: one person sees themselves at the centre of the world, and separate from their surroundings; the other sees themselves as intrinsically part of the landscape.

Watch someone from overseas learn to handpass: they balance the ball on the palm of their hand way out in front of themselves, then swing their arm at it like they are hitting a tennis forehand. Learning how to do it is like learning to roll the French *r* – to an English speaker it takes a counterintuitive leap. The sound is so unfamiliar it takes real concentration and effort to learn how to manipulate the tongue just right to produce the correct sound. And it's the same with learning how to kick, mark and handball.

But understanding football is not just like mastering another language. It is like mastering a different *type* of language, like a Westerner changing their thoughts radically enough that they can locate north in a dark cave. Learning the grammar and vocabulary of another language is one thing. Learning to think in a way that changes the whole conception of reality is another thing entirely.

Someone born speaking the language of football understands the flow of the game, the pattern of cause and effect, intuitively. For someone seeing football for the first time as an adult, learning to kick, mark and handball is difficult. But understanding the 'loosely organised chaos' of football at its most basic level – the way players move in concert with one another – represents the largest barrier a player must overcome to succeed at any level of football; learning how to master, to know it subconsciously, separates good players from truly great ones.

Alice

3.

Every Saturday morning, youth worker Jim Markovski runs the Redskins basketball team in RecWest, the local community centre in the western Melbourne suburb of Braybrook. The Redskins are a rag-tag group of kids who run around the basketball court in borrowed uniforms and not-the-latest KDs or LeBrons. They throw behind-the-back passes and dribble between their legs, but always within the confines of the team. No one gets angry when one of those behind-the-back passes flies out of bounds. Everyone understands that what they lack in organisation and support they make up for in physical flair.

The older kids are tall and lithe, and prowl around between games like jaguars, playfully springing up to slam-dunk. They have more or less the physical attributes of the recent American recruits at Collingwood, North Melbourne and St Kilda. They can *jump*. But unlike the American recruits, they already know how to play football. And although these other-worldly players are right here, in Braybrook, they might as well be on the other side of the world for the social and economic chasm that separates them from their sporting dreams.

The arena they play in has a sign that says 'Strictly no bouncing of balls in the foyer', but God help the person who tries to enforce that rule. By any statistical measure, Braybrook and the suburbs around it are some of the most disadvantaged in Victoria, according to the *Dropping off the Edge* report published by Catholic Social Services and Jesuit Social Services. Tracking 667 Victorian postcodes through indicators such as internet access, income, literacy, long-term unemployment, juvenile offending and criminal convictions, Braybrook almost won the wooden spoon.

But these kids still have footy dreams.

Atali Patrice is twelve, turning thirteen. He is tall for his age, with a quiet confidence, and his dark eyes shine when he explains how he got into AFL. 'One time, I came home from school and I started watching footy on telly.' No one explained the rules to him: 'I worked things out, what was happening. Then I asked my mum if I could play.'

He began playing for the Sunshine Kangaroos. They play against other teams in the western suburbs such as St Albans, Williamstown, Albion and Caroline Springs. The kids with African heritage, like Atali, already show signs of being built like NBA players – long, lithe and sprightly. And they can play multiple sports. These kids have discipline and drive, and a vague idea that they need some sort of agent or recruiter to notice them. These hopes may not be in vain, because some of the Redskins players have been so recognised, and gone on to professional basketball careers in the United States.

Atali prefers football over basketball because, he says, 'You can use every part of your body, not just your hands.' He trains twice a week by himself, but sometimes his friend Mike comes over. Mike is a sunny and confident young man of thirteen with a cheeky sitcom smile. 'I coach these guys, yeah, they're real good,' he tells us. 'They're not saying much but they're good.' We ask how Mike coaches his friends Joel and Baal, who is Atali's older brother. 'I make them run around, do passes, that sort of thing.'

If the AFL are looking for skilled players who are physically taller and can jump, this seems to be their place. But sadly, the increasing 'professionalism' of the game means that the recruiters are searching elsewhere, for a more ready-trained type of sportsperson. This might be the way of the future for the game – ever sleeker, more technically perfect, more television-savvy – but to understand the heartbeat of Australian football is to understand the game historically. AFL has always been linked to class and suburban tribalism, with supporters harbouring the kind of solidarity you'd find in a trade union movement. In fact, football is perhaps one of the clearest embodiments of Australian egalitarianism: a way for working class boys to not only achieve fortune and fame, but also a respect that transcends their class. In the arena, players are watched by doctors and delivery drivers, businessmen and builders alike.

The 1980s and 1990s saw a great deal of talent from the sons of Italian and Greek migrants, but the new global direction of this very local game means that athletes from all over the world can now play for the Western Bulldogs or Collingwood. It's true that Australians have also made it to the NBA (and other American leagues), but basketball is an international sport in a way that Australian football is not. The legendary youth worker, Les Twentyman, who has worked on the streets of Braybrook for decades, declares that: 'I am not convinced that their football club is the most important thing in the individual life of every football president, or coach or club captain. But for many supporters it is just that. Players and coaches and administrators can go off with other clubs; your average supporter can go nowhere.' Les mentions an older player of great promise when we ask if we could interview some of his at-risk kids who aspired to footy careers, but Les says that the young man is currently in jail: 'Football was the only thing he had going for him,' Les tells us sadly.

4.

Jim, who has worked in Braybrook for over thirty years, talks about the structural disadvantage faced by the kids he coaches:

> I was always told 'Braybrook's kids are no hopers', fairly disadvantaged and you can't plant trees because they've got total disrespect. There were no trees, the roads were terrible, there was no infrastructure and nowhere for young people to do anything or have an outlet. I pride myself and challenged myself to say, 'No, that's crap because all young people need to do is to be loved, valued and listened to.'[2]

Les and Jim decided that organising sporting teams would help diffuse gang formation by allowing kids to channel their energy into competition instead of violence, and they take these young sportspeople seriously. We watch the boys tease each other and get ready for their next game. They joke around, but when it comes time to play, they play in earnest. There is none of that serious, hostile competitiveness that comes from parental pressure – these boys' parents drop them off at the centre; many don't even speak English let alone understand the language of football. Yet Atali, Baal, Joel and Mike – these kids are all native speakers trying to live out their dreams.

---

1. Guy Deutscher, *Through the Language Glass: Why the World Looks Different in Other Languages*, Henry Holt & Company, 2010, p.172.
2. Interview with Jim Markovski, *The Westsider*, 1 July 2015.

The Warm Up

EMMA
How's everyone feeling?

FELICITY
Better now that I've thrown up.

LUCY
Nervous. Doing circle work in the lounge room.

EMMA
I'm lining shit up. Clothes for tonight, tomorrow, passes, Myki, glasses...

FELICITY
Feeling decidedly normal now. Bless you all.

EMMA
...Banana lounge and sleeping bag...

KATE
As Ben Lee reminds us, we are all in this together.

EMMA
I just did my first nervous poo.

MARNGROOK

Maxine Beneba Clarke

back when / songlines hummed a way
through grey-gum
(which was not yet called grey-gum)
back when / spirits spilled
from salty inlets / that i
have no traditional name or right
or tongue
          for
way dreamtime black
before the bloodshed

there was marngrook:
gunditjmara game ball

a warrior's sport
of thought / stealth
and speed

marngrook

barefoot winged brown
bodies stretching so high
through the sky / legend
says / some of those men
could fly

before football
there wz *marngrook*

it made wise men / and warriors
of the boys / of this land

and this land is not mine
but if i understand

marngrook

there were also games
the white men took / and
changed / in my land
400 years ago / someone
with my blood / and
my fire / and my face

who gave birth to someone / who
gave birth to someone
who gave birth to someone / who gave

birth to me

was chained
and stolen
too

i do not know the name
of the game
that she played / but
i want to say

marngrook

when the national
anthem plays / and
i'm high up in the bleachers

i watch those men
whose blood is land / i
see them stand / heart
under hand / and sing
i see / the flicker
in their eyes / i
watch their chests rise
up and down
and wonder

how anyone in this stadium
can breathe

australians all let us rejoice
for we are young
and free

as if it/s not enough to stand
on stolen land / and sing
in joyful strains

as if it's not enough / to play
a stolen game / before the colonisers
who deny its name / as if
it/s not enough
a thirteen year old child
decides to really put you
in your place

it/s may 26 / 2013
the Indigenous round / of the afl
the sun is shining
the stands are packed

the stadium is awash with red

white
and black

at the end of this game
sydney will have
wupped collingwood / by

a mammoth forty seven points

it is 136 in the 4th
sydney 96 to 54
goodes is heading / for
the boundary line
6 lean foot / of 2 time
brownlow 4 time
all australian / proud
indigenous swan

20 years after winmar lifted
up his shirt & pointed
at his skin
in the indigenous round
dedicated to him / goodes
hears a voice echo / in the wind

ape / aaaaape
it says
and goodes turns / strides to
the front row / points

and a 13 year old child
is disgraced / before
the country

and the country sees its

own 13 year old face

and the world is broadcast
the adolescent race hate
of a nation

my children / are
playing lego
on the lounge room floor
and the game / is still rolling / but i
don't want to play this anymore

i don't want to belong
in a country of people
whose ancestors slayed
half-continents / but
who still can't understand
that ignorance is hate

i don't want to be part
of a generation / of parents
teaching their children
to *un-know* what it is / to point
to a black man / & say *ape*

i / want to know
the black nation
that could raise a man

of such metal / he could point
these cold facts out
in the harsh light of day
to a braying marngrook stadium

the commentators have always said
it is football
we / don/t know a thing
about this so-called

'marngrook'

the commentators started saying
how can a thirteen year old child / be held
responsible for what it is
she did

the commentators / they
are raising / our thirteen year old kids

the commentators gave us
new aussie rules
and now a game that made wise
brown men / of young brown boys

can also crown kings / from fools

the truth is: we are only ever as much
as what we teach our children

and so many of our children
have got it wrong

ask your child
do they know / about marngrook
nuh uh
marn what?
but every single one of
them has a club / and a scarf
and a song

we are what we teach our children
and our children
are wrong

shame

if adam goodes taught us anything
on that field / on that day

it's no matter
who we are / no matter
where we are / no matter who
or how many / are watching

it is always
marngrook:

gunditjmara
game
ball

it is our
responsibility
to point

LOVE & FOOTY

Christos Tsiolkas

In the early '80s, while the VFL grand final was on, the streets of Melbourne's CBD seemed the quietest place on earth. I loved it: the blanket of hush over the buildings, the empty and desolate winter streets, and most of all, the blessed freedom that for a few hours I could escape the gaze of family, school and peers. For three years, between the ages of fourteen and sixteen, I would select a film, take the train into the city, and make my way to the cinema. I would be the only one at the screening. Do I remember the films themselves? I am certain that one year it was Tim Burstall's *The Last of the Knucklemen*; so wildly inappropriate, of course – this was a film about uber-Ocker outback miners and here I was, committing sacrilege against an entrenched Aussie tradition. Did I watch Neil Simon's *Chapter Two* one year? Or Warren Beatty's *Reds*? I am convinced I saw Woody Allen's *Manhattan* during the 1980 grand final: it was a film

I watched obsessively that year, returning to it again and again, seduced by its black and white love-letter to a sophisticate New York. One day I'd leave the suburbs far behind, I promised myself. One day that would be me walking down the Upper West Side's avenues and streets, being witty, being philosophical, falling in love.

I *must* have seen *Manhattan* on grand final day, 1980. I must have.

Football was always around in my childhood. I was introduced to both codes, to the *real* football, soccer, by my Greek immigrant father; and to the local code, Aussie Rules, almost by osmosis: through the schoolyard, through trading cards, through television, and through only living a few blocks back from the Punt Road Oval. It was inconceivable that I would barrack for any other team than Richmond. That was where I lived and that was whom you followed; there was no question of barracking for anyone else. I had friends who lived on the Abbotsford side of Victoria Street, a five-minute walk from home, and they were staunchly Collingwood. My cousins, who lived in Burnley, near the river, had to choose between Richmond and Hawthorn. The borders of my childhood were parochial and fixed. I could only be for the Tigers.

I didn't have the physique or the talent for soccer. It is a sublime game, still the most balletic of the football codes.

But Aussie Rules was an easier game to play, especially for an overweight kid. Possibly if I had grown up in New South Wales or in Queensland I would have found my sport in rugby. I didn't mind smashing through a crowd of boys; I excelled at British Bulldog. But I couldn't manage that fearlessness when it came to either soccer or footy. I didn't have the gracefulness or the doggedness required to pursue the ball; and even if I did manage to mark it or have it passed to me, I couldn't think fast enough when it came to disposing of it or kicking it on. In the schoolyard I always found myself either in the forward line or the ruck; in both positions I could elbow my way to the ball, bring a smaller opponent down. But I was pretty useless once I did get it. To this day I have sympathy for the player who goes off-side, or has the crowd screaming furiously at them, 'Ball!' The embarrassed shrug of their shoulders, their refusal to look out to the crowd, the spitting out of an expletive: I know exactly how they feel.

Maybe footy won over soccer because it was so damn ubiquitous: it was always on the television, on the radio. The players' profiles and faces were on the swap-cards in gum packets; it seemed to take up half of the *Sun* and the *Herald*. It was everywhere. Soccer, during that first wave of post-WWII immigration, was staunchly ethnic. My dad was South Melbourne Hellas. But my friends were Serb and Croat, Turkish and Italian as well as Greek, and so our tribe became Richmond. Maybe that, more than any other reason, made footy *our* game in the way that soccer could never be. Not back then. We would all meet on the corner of Punt Road and Bridge Road, sling our arms around each other, make our way across the park to the MCG and barrack unanimously for one side, *our* side, Richmond. That ardent support for football, as well as our sharing of the English language, marked us out as different from our parents: it made us Australian.

I loved footy, I loved it with a child's unselfconscious passion.

My best friend at primary school was named after an apostle and I adored him. He loved footy and he excelled at it. He seemed to have an endless supply of Richmond team jumpers and singlets, and he would wear them every day at school, winter or summer. He would wear them at home and he would wear the singlet for pyjamas when going to bed. He was wiry and tough, and he'd inherited dirty blond hair from his Macedonian mother and glistening olive skin from his Peloponnesian father. But try as I might I can't recollect the rest of his features: not his mouth or his eyes, not his face. I remember the speed of his attack on the ball, and I can recall the smell of those footy shirts; an intoxicating perfume, boy sweat and the chemical sharpness of the Omo laundry detergent all our mothers used. When we played footy I always wanted to be on the other team so I could hurl myself at him. He'd always evade my clumsy tackle, slip away from my embrace and run off with the ball, kicking it towards the goals, turning back in delight to poke out his tongue or to shout out some teasing abuse. I would just laugh and laugh. It was bliss to see him so happy.

We would touch each other all the time. I can close my eyes and remember the weight of his arm around my shoulders as we crouched under the eucalypt at North Richmond Primary School, trading footy cards with the other boys. Each day we sat next to each other in class, and sometimes we held hands. It was in Grade Four, crammed over our maths book, struggling over some exercise, our heads touching, his arm around me, when he suddenly jerked back in delight at conquering the equation. He was euphoric with pride, the same fire in his eyes as when he kicked a goal. I leaned into him and kissed him on the mouth. His joy was unabated until we heard our teacher shout out our names. She was standing over us, scowling.

'You two are disgusting.'

I think that was the first time I felt shame. All the other kids were staring at us. One of the girls began to giggle and one of the boys called out, 'They're poofters miss, they *leurve* each other.'

My friend sprung up from his seat, his stance, his fury, daring the other boy. 'I'm not a fucking poofter!'

Our teacher came up beside him. 'Sit down,' she said quietly but firmly. 'And we do not use such foul language.'

My friend sat down but was teetering at the edge of our shared bench. I didn't know where to look, I didn't know what to say. I felt dirty but I knew that I couldn't cry, I mustn't cry. I felt so filthy and so ugly.

Not long after, during a lunchtime game of footy, I tackled him once more and once more fumbled the ball. He didn't dance off, he didn't turn back to playfully taunt me. He just spat out, 'Jeez, Tsiolkas, you're bloody hopeless.'

In Grade Five he had a new best friend. And so did I. But I knew not to touch him. I knew I had to keep my physical distance.

I hated football, I fucking hated it.

It wasn't just that dangerous kiss that turned me away from football. My parents, like so many migrants, decided to flee the inner city and in Year Eight I ended up in a school where only a handful of us came from Southern Europe, Asia or the Balkans. Soccer was wog-ball and nobody played it, and you didn't barrack for a footy team based on any territorial loyalty but because your nanna or grandfather had once upon a time lived in Essendon. It wasn't just the kiss and it wasn't just the move away from my old friends. I had slowly but deliberately begun to fashion another identity for myself. I had always loved reading and films but now I was determinedly literary and consciously a cinephile. At this new school, my best friends were girls not boys, and we all shared an antipathy towards sport. It marked us out as different. Sport was for dickheads and conservatives. Sport was sexist. We called ourselves feminists and socialists and our espousal of such beliefs made us a distinct tribe. All these changes didn't happen overnight; they emerged gradually and painfully. Difference wasn't respected back then and it certainly wasn't celebrated. We were weirdos and commies and poofters and lezzos and freaks and dags. Maybe that's why Woody Allen's *Manhattan* meant so much to us. We were stuck in the boring and narrow-minded suburbs, but one day we would be walking the streets and avenues of the Upper West Side, talking art and politics. We'd never come back to Melbourne. Fucking never ever.

We were a cliché as well, but we were young and so, of course, we didn't know it.

The best football player at our school had the surname of a fine bourbon whiskey. He was strong, tall and had rough Celtic features. I had already made that vow to ignore the grand final, to seek out movies on the day to demonstrate the full force of my loathing. But I knew the game: you can't erase knowledge, and I knew enough to pick who were the best players. It was *he* who was swiftest, the most cunning and the most courageous. It was a secret thrill to watch him play. In three years I don't think I said a word to him even though we were in the same class. I didn't speak to him but I had memorised every inch of his body. In the locker rooms, after PE, after a game, I would try not to look at him. But it was impossible to look away. The long legs, the rigid tendons on them; the light spray of golden tight curls on his navel; the shocking white of his buttocks and the long slant of his cock.

In our final year at high school, our teacher divided us into groups one day to discuss *Pride and Prejudice*. My binder was pasted with images I had cut out from magazines: Jane Fonda giving the Vietcong salute, Diane Keaton in *Annie Hall*, the famous still of Jean Marais kissing his reflection in *Orpheus*, and a young Fidel Castro. The boy with the name that made me want to get drunk on bourbon was sitting next to me, his grey school slacks so tight they were frayed white at the crotch, when he leaned across and whispered, 'So you barrack for Richmond, eh?'

On the corner of the inside cover, amid the revolutionary heroes and the silver screen stars, I had stuck a photograph of Kevin Bartlett. Somehow, in that unconscious but deliberate way we lie to ourselves, I had not been able to part with that image of one of the greatest players in the history of Australian Rules Football. His feats on the field were heroic, and for those of us who had Richmond in the blood, he was unquestionably a hero. Every summer, without my registering it, I had peeled the sticker off my previous year's English binder and attached it to the collage for the new year. The sticker was torn, scratched and smudged with ink. But I hadn't thrown it away. I hadn't got rid of it. The boy winked at me, his grin cheerful and friendly, taking my silence for assent.

'Me too,' he said. 'We've always barracked for the Tigers.'

My sudden consciousness that my leg was touching his frightened me. I deliberately shifted away from him.

We did become friends. And I did fall in love, not that I ever dared tell him.

Changes rarely happen overnight. They sometimes do: I am thinking of the devastating cold shock of accident and sudden death, of suicide; I have been witness to two friends falling in love at first sight. But mostly, change creeps up on us slowly, taking years to announce itself. I didn't don the Richmond colours and start attending games, not for some while. That final year of high school I went to the movies on grand final day. But I started to glance at the sports pages again. I didn't turn away from the television when a game was on. I felt the resurgence of pride as Richmond stormed its way to the finals, recalled every word of *our* song, the best football anthem in the whole of the world. I did catch that wave at high tide that brought myself – and gentrification – back to the inner city but I have never lived in Manhattan. I fell deeply and reciprocally in love with a boy who barracked for St Kilda. His immigrant father, just like mine, preferred soccer, *real* football, to Aussie Rules. I started attending footy matches, hosting grand final barbeques, and when money came my way, I became a member of *my* club.

I have one small regret about that long-ago place called adolescence, about being a gay youth at a time when homosexuality was illegal, shameful and silenced, when masculinity and femininity were still rigidly policed and self-policed: that I did not attend those games when the Richmond Football Club were the champions of the VFL. I missed out. And there is a trace of irrational paranoia every time I watch Richmond play, that my presence dooms them, that they'll lose the match, that their good fortune in the late '70s and early '80s had something to do with my decision to look away.

In my mid twenties, at an airport lounge at Tullamarine, waiting for a delayed flight, I looked across from my seat to where a man was whispering to his wife, their daughter impatiently banging her legs against the seat, their son jumping on and off his. He had grown a moustache, he had put on a little weight, but it was undoubtedly my friend from high school. I went up to him, and on recognising me, he rose and gave me a strong hug. I took in the sweet aroma of his cologne and his sweat. He introduced me to his family, and we chatted about the places our lives had taken us to.

'Still playing footy?' I asked him.

'Chris barracks for the Tigers,' he explained to his wife.

'Me too!' His daughter, for the first time, smiled up at me.

My friend turned back to me. 'No, mate, I wasn't that good.' He paused, then added, cheekily: 'But so much better than you.'

And he winked, and again, that warmth, that friendliness; and for a moment, my heart swelled. How good it felt and how much it hurt. But it only lasted a moment, and in the next breath we were continuing our small talk and not long after, their flight to Brisbane was called. We said our goodbyes, we hugged once more, and I returned to my seat. Watching him walk away I noticed he still wore his trousers tight, that his buttocks were still firm, his legs still long and strong.

Footballers. I have admired them and I have loved them, and for part of my life I hated them. Nowadays, watching them play, whether at the MCG or at the footy oval in Preston, best mates playing kick to kick on the beach at Mordialloc, I still think them the most beautiful creatures in the world.

I still want to kiss them on the mouth.

THE CALM SUPPORTER

Honey Brown

We exist. You'll find us way back in the outer, our club colours subtle, our hands warm around a coffee or a tea, our posture peaceable, our breathing steady, our eyes shifting to and from the game. We're known to turn away at the most critical moments – a mark fifty out with only seconds on the clock, a roll-of-the-dice boundary throw-in just before the siren, a ball-up inside the goal square. Crucial plays are best not witnessed, not by us; the groan of the crowd, or the cheer, is quite enough.

We go for food when the game gets too electric. A soggy salad wrap, less-than-fresh sushi, uninspiring chips, or the much-maligned pie; these things seriously mulled over and chosen, while the ground throbs and the crowd howls. You'll catch us doing a three-quarter-time tour of the stadium, strolling down the vacant corridors, glimpsing the recommencement of play, filtering it, using the great slabs of

Southern Stand concrete as our buffer.

Ready again, we reintegrate, still sticking to the back stalls though, our arms folded, chin lifted, shoulder to shoulder with those less controlled compatriots, the ones breathing through their teeth and clawing at their scalp. Poor bastards. *Our* blood pressure remains steady; we fix a small, rueful smile on our lips, because we know – win or lose, we'll be okay. Granted, our gaze is, perhaps, a touch unfocused, and when we swallow it is dry and deep, and we may, or may not, avoid all eye contact and conversation. Calm though, all the same. We don't swear. We don't curse. We inhale. Exhale. Breathe.

A one-finger beat might start up against our thigh, as we tap out an easy-listening tune, blocking that feral chant of the opposition's cheer squad. Better to cluck your tongue when the ball hits the post than to shred your larynx in a scream, better to wet your lips when a favourite player is run down and tackled than to spray spittle on everyone around you, better to rub your hands at the umpire's whistle than to throw both hands forward, pointing, clenching, threatening, wildly shaking, *Are you for fucking real?*

Breathe. Inhale. Exhale.

We turn our attention to the cold, gusting wind, do up the top button on our coat, brush the chip salt from our sleeve. Nowadays we can even Tweet/Insta/Facebook our untroubled ease – *#alwaysnextseason*. And it's true, we do steer our thoughts to the future, even while witnessing a win slide away. We veer oh-so-smoothly from present to … any goddamn future fucking game but this one.

Inhale. Exhale.

A young side rebuilding. Positives to be taken. New players finding their feet. We have intergenerational Love of Club to fall back on. It's woven into our DNA. It's a team-coloured double helix. From birth we've been zipped into our club onesie, booties knitted by Nan, old-school VFL badge beanie handed down from Pop, collectable membership pins and paraphernalia to be treasured. We've been blooded by cousins, eyed for loyalty by uncompromising aunts, battle-readied by uncles; no wriggle room, not when 'Team' is this entrenched and the lineage unbroken. And no desire to wriggle free either. Our team. Blind faith. Tradition. Not even a shift interstate will sway us. Rip us from mainland (heartland), ship us across Bass Strait (well before the Hawks had claimed the Island State), and place us, as youngsters, in front of a classroom full of confused fellow students, mystified by our Victorian uniform of an oversized guernsey, tasselled scarf, desert boots and duffle coat; drop us in this Collingwood-barren alien landscape, and watch us stay true, never abate. (Disregarding our teenage madness, the adolescent lure to the dark side, a.k.a the gaudy yellow and blue of the newcomers West Coast, and only in bed with the devil for one wild high school footy-themed disco night, when all that mattered was what outfit best complemented blue mascara.)

Displaced, tested, deprived, we return to homeland, to country, re-embraced into the temper tantrums, tears, beers and shouting. Decades of wins and losses, the ebbs and flows, the highs and lows, the ups and downs tempering us, mellowing us – only natural it does. A wise supporter sees it for the long march it is. We pace ourselves. We settle down. We fall in.

Proof of regiment comes in the final-quarter comeback, that sudden and unexpected goal haul, the senior players standing up, the midfielders finding top gear, the opposition stunned and stumbling, and the offending cheer squad chant stopping dead ... *Feel the burn*, *bloody mongrels*, *not so vocal now!* ... Others might say. Not us.

We're the calm ones. What excites many won't ruffle us. Another cup of tea? Chai latte? When the crowd surges forward we step further back. Time for a chocolate bar, no hurry, off to the vending machine situated in the most isolated of stadium spots, the one spied on our earlier food reconnaissance mission. We expertly decipher the crowd's groans and gasps; we can judge the jeers from the cheers, yelps from the yowls, all the while, our heart not pounding much, not tight through the chest and no need to un-crink our neck or roll our shoulders.

Calm.

Violet Crumble. Or Peppermint Crisp? Chocolate contemplated while a hush descends, the eerie silence of 60,000 stilled footy souls, each one praying, depending on allegiance, for heavenly intervention. Even the ground staff caught in the intensity of it, pausing beside their mop buckets and brooms, looking to the monitors. But we don't have to look, not us. We know – it's our star full-forward tucking away his mouthguard, tightening his laces, about to straighten. We love him, but … he's not the league's straightest kick. So we unwrap our Violet Crumble and we avert our faces. We don't stare, dry-eyed, transfixed, as the game reaches its zenith, that nerve-strumming crescendo, that be-all and end-all of what the commentators have decided is the absolute make-or-break moment of the entire football season …

Instead, we bite down.

You *could*, I guess, liken it to biting down on a piece of leather fastened between our teeth, while our strapped and secured body bucks, muscles twitch, eyelids flutter. But it's a chocolate bar, for Christ's sake. Chill. The kick misses. The opposition's feral chant resumes. Momentum swings away. And we chew honeycomb and chocolate. That's how it's done, you see. Unaffected. Totally okay. Totally.

You won't see us cutting and running early. No need. We're there until the end, final siren, game over, not a problem, opposition club song blaring, good on 'em, so what. Not bothered. Nope. We're already reconciled on the way through the gates, at peace by the time we hit the car park. We cut a clean line through the exhausted, depleted and destroyed. We move confidently, wise and mature, the grown-up supporters, the adults within the ranks, leaving the ground in the same manner in which we arrived – content within our unshakable faith.

Ready to return again next season, full of untarnished hope.

That's us getting behind the wheel of our car, good to go, a certain tension, perhaps, some effort bending, stiff spine, tiny bit of trouble sitting down, buckling in, reaching for the ignition, scarf too tight, jacket too heavy, a few issues … breathing.

Inhale.

Exhale.

A slight whimper.

We are the muffled cries inside our cars. You've spotted us thrashing about, thumping the wheel, elbowing the window, kneeing the dash. We're the ones you've paused for on your way past, kindly resting your hand on the car bonnet, giving our bumper a tap. Commiserations. Because *you* know there is no such thing as a calm supporter. Try as we might.

I CAN TELL YOU HOW ADAM GOODES FEELS. EVERY INDIGENOUS PERSON HAS FELT IT

Stan Grant

I have wondered for days if I should say anything about Adam Goodes.

My inclination is to look for common ground, to be diplomatic. Some of the fault is with Adam. Maybe he's been unnecessarily provocative. Racism? Perhaps. Perhaps the crowds just don't like him.

Yes, I could make a case for all of that. But there are enough people making those arguments and all power to them.

Here's what I can do. I can tell you what it is like for us. I can tell you what Adam must be feeling, because I've felt it. Because every Indigenous person I know has felt it.

It may not be what you want to hear. Australians are proud of their tolerance yet can be perplexed when challenged on race, their response often defensive.

I may be overly sensitive. I may see insult where none is intended. Maybe my position of relative success and privilege today should have healed deep scars of racism and the pain of growing up Indigenous in Australia. The same could be said of Adam. And perhaps that is right.

But this is how Australia makes us feel. Estranged in the land of our ancestors, marooned by the tides of history on the fringes of one of the richest and demonstrably most peaceful, secure and cohesive nations on earth.

The 'wealth for toil' we praise in our anthem has remained out of our reach. Our position at the bottom of every socio-economic indicator tragically belies the Australian economic miracle.

'Australians all let us rejoice' can ring hollow to us. Ours is more troubled patriotism. Our allegiance to Australia, our pride in this country undercut by the dark realities of our existence.

Seeds of suspicion and mistrust are planted early in the Indigenous child. Stories of suffering, humiliation and racism told at the feet of our parents and grandparents feed an identity that struggles to reconcile a pride in heritage with the forlorn realities of a life of defeat.

From childhood I often cringed against my race. To be Aboriginal was to be ashamed. Ashamed of our poverty. Ashamed of the second-hand clothes with the giveaway smell of mothballs and another boy's name on the shirt collar.

Ashamed of the way my mother and grandmother had to go to the Smith Family or Salvation Army for food vouchers. Ashamed of the onions and mince that made up too many meals.

We were ashamed of the bastardised wreckage of a culture that we clung to. This wasn't the Dreamtime. This was mangy dogs and broken glass.

Like the Goodes family, we moved constantly as my father chased work. But wherever we went we found our place always on the fringes. What semblance of pride we carried too easily laid low by a mocking glance or a schoolyard joke.

We were the blacks. So easily recognised not just by the colour of our skin but by the whiff of desperation and danger we cloaked ourselves in. What resentment we harboured, we too often turned on ourselves, played out in wild scrambling brawls from the playground to the showgrounds that sent the same message: stay away from the blacks.

There was humour and there was love and there was survival. And as I grew older I pieced together the truth that we didn't choose this. We are the detritus of the brutality of the Australian frontier.

As Australia welcomed waves of migrants and built a rich, diverse, tolerant society, we remained a reminder of what was lost, what was taken, what was destroyed to scaffold the building of this nation's prosperity.

We survived the 'smoothing of the dying pillow' of extermination to end up on the bottom rung of the ladder of assimilation. Too many of us remain there still. Look to the statistics: the worst health, housing, education, the lowest life expectancy, highest infant mortality. An Indigenous youth has more chance of being locked up than educated.

If good fortune or good genes means you are among the lucky few to find an escape route then you face a choice: to 'go along to get along', mind your manners, count your blessings and hide in the comfort of the Australian dream; or to infuse your success with an indignation and a righteousness that will demand this country does not look away from its responsibilities and its history.

I found a path through education that led to journalism. A love of knowledge and an inquisitiveness that has shot me through with anger. A deeper understanding of history, of politics, of economics, leaving me resentful of our suffering.

I wrestle with that anger as the boy I was wrestled with his shame. I want to see the good in a society that defies the history of its treatment of my people.

It is the legacy of my grandfather who signed up to fight a war for a country that didn't recognise his humanity, let alone his citizenship. It is the lesson of the example of the lives of my mother and father, my uncles and aunties. Lives of decency and hard work and responsibility and rooted in our identity as Indigenous Australians.

When I was sixteen I summoned the courage to speak to my class. As the only Indigenous kid, the only Aboriginal person my schoolmates had met, I wanted to tell my family's story. My teacher was proud and encouraging. When class returned after lunch the words 'be kind to abos' were scrawled across the blackboard.

The rejection, the humiliation, cut me to the core.

This is the journey too of Adam Goodes. A man whose physical gifts have set him above and given him a platform available to so few and whose courage demands that he use it to speak to us all.

Events in recent years have sent Adam on a quest to understand the history of his people, to challenge stereotypes and perceptions. I have spoken to him about this. I recognise in him the same quest I see in myself. It is a conversation I have had with so many of my Indigenous brothers and sisters.

This is rare air for anyone, let alone a footballer. He has faltered at times and the expression of his anger at our history and his pride in his identity has been challenging, if not divisive.

The events of 2013 when he called out a thirteen-year-old girl for a racial taunt opened a wound that has only deepened. To some the girl was unfairly vilified. Adam's war dance of this year challenged and scared some people. His talent, the way he plays the game, alienates others.

And now we have this, a crescendo of boos. The racial motivation of some giving succour to the variously defined hatred of others.

To Adam's ears, the ears of so many Indigenous people, these boos are a howl of humiliation. A howl that echoes across two centuries of invasion, dispossession and suffering. Others can parse their words and look for other explanations, but we see race and only race. How can we see anything else when race is what we have clung to even as it has been used as a reason to reject us.

I found refuge outside Australia. My many years working in Asia, the Middle East, Europe and Africa liberated me. Here were the problems of other peoples and other lands. Here I was an observer freed from the shackles of my own country's history.

I still wonder if it would be easier to leave again.

But people – like Adam Goodes, other Indigenous sportsmen and women who are standing with him, his non-Indigenous teammates and rivals who support him, and my non-Indigenous wife, my children and their friends of all colours and the people of goodwill who don't have the answers but want to keep asking questions of how we can all be better – maybe they all make it worth staying.

HOW TO LOVE FOOTBALL

Anna Spargo-Ryan

1

THROW

In his life, my grandfather deeply loved only three things: his church, his wife, and the Norwood Redlegs. The first was of no interest to me, but the other two were inextricably linked.

The autumn I was eight, Gramps taught me to play football. Not deliberately, of course. He was the kind of man who thought girls shouldn't do much of anything. Girls were for raising children and going shopping and definitely not for playing football.

By the time I was born, he was already old. He was tall, bean-like. His limbs were longer than necessary and he sort of threw them around as he walked. He put salt on everything, including on other salt. He had huge hands, swollen from many years of toil, and he put them around me and discovered I was a baby, not a lettuce – a constant source of confusion for him.

But he was a soft, loping man. A simple, admiring, respectful man.

He smiled often. Mostly when he thought people couldn't see him. He was the kind of man who would stand in a doorjamb and watch the way other people were with one another, and be delighted by it. He was careful and considered, but clumsy. He worked to keep his mind sharp by adding lists of numbers and calculating compound interest. He spent time in his toolshed and he ate Eskimo Pies and he showed my brother how to look for velvet geckos under the broken tiles in the wall.

My gramps was mostly quiet in his joy. He was a quiet fan of his black and white cat, Champs. He was a quiet fan of a particular stone bench near the fishponds in his garden. He was a quiet fan of tinkering on his Wurlizter organ.

He was, more than anything, a patient man. And it was because of this that I learned to love football.

2

BALL

That year, Gramps and Nanna began taking me into town for a Saturday afternoon strudel bun in Kappy's Cafe. If I was really good we would go to Haigh's on Beehive Corner, and Nanna would buy me a single chocolate in a silver box. Afterwards we walked close to the river, where we could sometimes hear the cheers go up at Adelaide Oval, or stand and watch the streams of colour pour from the gates.

But it wasn't as straightforward as that.

You see, these accidental lessons took place not on a footy oval, as you might imagine, but in the back of a red Datsun 120Y.

It was, frankly, a shitbox. On warm afternoons I had to peel my skin away from the black vinyl seats; on cold ones, rain slapped at the rusted metal and froze us in place. The doors thudded in their hinges and the windows only wound down halfway before they were on such a lean they couldn't go any further.

But Gramps loved that car. It contained the only source of entertainment he ever needed: ABC Adelaide 891.

The first Saturday outing took place on a blustery Adelaide Hills day, wind coming up Greenhill Road and into the carport. There was no AFL then, not yet, but I had inherited from my dad an obligation to support the world's worst team – the South Adelaide Panthers – and that was a source of much delight (and gloating) for Gramps. Nanna had waved us from the house, promising to 'be there in a minute!' in her cake-soaked voice.

I believed her. I had never experienced the long wait.

We got in. Him: long limbs folded into the minute front

seat. Me: short legs and six different security toys buckled into the back.

And we waited.

And we waited, and we waited.

My nanna passed to my mother and then to me a particular penchant for neurosis. I'm not taking creative licence in telling you that on that day it took two hours for Nanna to triple-check every power point, every light switch. We had enough time, stuck to those vinyl seats, to listen to an entire game of football. I don't know which it was. That was the thing about Gramps – although he was a diehard Norwood supporter, he would listen to any match from any ground. He loved his Redlegs, but more than that, he loved the game.

And so, he listened. It was white noise to me, the monotonous voices calling strings of unfamiliar names. Words I had no action for. The radio crackled and popped and half the time was spent tuning and re-tuning and re-re-tuning. I was bored, desperate for strudel bun.

But then, something magical happened. My introverted, observant, reverent grandfather got angry. He got loud. He slammed his fists on the steering wheel. He blurted and hollered and huffed and at one point he sat straight up in his seat and his hair touched the roof of the tiny red car and he shouted: '*Holding the ball!*' and his face was damp and shiny.

I was giddy with this new Gramps, this animated and hysterical Gramps.

Nanna got in the car. She flicked the radio off. The spell was broken.

We went into town and to Kappy's Cafe for a strudel bun, and down Rundle Mall to the Balfour's Cafe, because one cafe was never enough cafes. There we sat in the mirrored hall and poked forks into green frog cakes and I thought, *What was that thing Gramps said, about holding the ball?* It had seemed very important.

We went home in the car and Nanna cut me slices of apple and wiped my feet with a warm cloth before bed. From the spare bedroom I looked at his shoulders hunched over a world atlas in the study. *Holding the ball.* If anything, it seemed like the kind of thing a person *should* do, in a game of football.

I had to wait a whole week to find out. Outside of the car, Gramps was his other self. He did word-finds at the dining room table, fried a sausage in a tiny pan, talked to the cat perched on the arm of the couch.

But he did not mention football.

The following Saturday afternoon, we went once again to Kappy's Cafe. 'I'll be down in a minute!' Nanna said. I knew what to expect. I looked forward to it. We got into the car, let our skin schloop into the black vinyl, and the radio clunked on. *It's a beautiful afternoon down here at*

Norwood Oval. And it was, even in the carport. Adelaide autumn, clear and cool and bright. A horn sounded. People cheered. I looked to Gramps to see the change in his face.

'Carn Nords!' he shouted. 'Get it down!' He fumed and hissed and puffed. Thumped the wheel. Thumped the window. 'Holding the ball!'

There it was again. 'What does that mean?' I asked him. 'Holding the ball?'

He stopped. Looked at me. Looked at the radio. Brought his face very close to mine as though imparting a wonderful secret. I leaned close, too, waited for this information that would surely change everything.

'It means,' he said, in his rumbling baritone, 'that the player had prior opportunity to dispose of the ball, but didn't do so before he was tackled.'

'Oh,' I said. 'I get it.' And I peeled my skin from the vinyl seats to listen more closely. Waited for someone to hold the ball so I could figure out what he'd just said. Knowing but not understanding the significance of what he had shared.

My education continued into winter. I gave Nanna reasons to take even longer to get ready – leaving the heater on, putting the cat outside. She would flap around the house and I would run to the car, cram myself into the backseat and let the rusted door thud. I began to look forward not to the strudel buns but to the familiar lilt of Ken Cunningham calling the match.

'What's the score?' I would ask, and Gramps would tune it again and we would wait until someone scored or for three-quarter time and he would tell me: 'Six goals up,' or 'Three points down,' and I would say, 'Oooh,' and forget to ask which team was winning.

'Did they give him a free?' I would ask. 'Did it go out of bounds?' and he would turn to look at me, right in the eye, and offer explanations steeped in science and tradition.

He started to bring scraps of paper with him, to illustrate what I needed to know. Here's a half-forward flank. Here's where the full-forward stands. Here's where the teams go into their rooms to get shouted at by the coach.

One afternoon we waited through a thunderstorm. The carport flooded; rain came in through the cracked seals. Lightning added to the drama of it, the crash and bang of it, heads colliding, men tackled face-first into the mud. Nanna's verandah was slippery in the rain so she sat by the window until the clouds had passed and she apologised as she flicked off the radio but there was no need; that day I had learned 'worm burner'.

3
DELIBERATE

In 1993 the Redlegs played the Weagles in the SANFL grand final. It had been a tough couple of years for the club – with the formation of the Adelaide Crows AFL team it had lost many of its best players, and wallowed near the bottom of the ladder. It was Neil Craig who lifted them up again. Neil Craig, former Norwood great himself. Neil Craig, who would later be inducted into the South Australian Football hall of fame.

I knew all kinds of rules by then. In fact, I thought I knew every rule. Dad had informed me that I was a one-eyed Geelong Cats supporter, so I watched them play game after game, shouting the words I had learned in the back of the Datsun. I shouted 'Holding the man!' and 'Ball!' and 'That's a throw!' and I was ten years old and my passion for the game was incomparable, as far as I knew.

On that Saturday afternoon in October, Nanna made melting moments with lemon icing in the middle, and the three of us sat in their lounge room to watch the match. Nanna only ever lasted a few minutes, caught up then in feeding the magpies or dusting the curtains, but I was a stayer. Gramps could count on me. I was there, on their scratchy floral couch, until the final siren.

It did not go well. Gramps roared and he steamed and he blew smoke from his ears but it did not make a lick of difference. Time and again the ball came into the Weagles' fifty, sailed down the middle. I ate biscuits with my guts in my chest, watching his face, watching and waiting and hoping.

'Ball!' I shouted, watching for his reaction. 'Holding the man! Deliberate!' He didn't look at me once.

The Woodville-West Torrens Eagles smashed Norwood by 73 points that day.

Gramps stood, six-foot-two, knees cracking, and announced we would be going out for dinner. Nanna said, 'I'll be down in a minute!' and he and I went to the carport, climbed into the red Datsun.

And we waited.

And we waited, and we waited.

He didn't turn the radio on. Just sat there with the wipers going, through minute after minute of excruciating silence.

I said, 'What happened?' and he said, 'Shhhh.' And so I learned a new rule after all: the rule where you had to be silent some of the time.

4
SHEPHERD

They found out Gramps had cancer by accident. That was the way of him, bumping into things. He went to Darwin to visit my uncle, and while he was there his feet swelled up so much he couldn't wear shoes. They all laughed. He went to the hospital and nurses took his blood. And they found cancer in it.

He was okay, for a while. It was early, slow-growing. Nanna moved faster to get out of the house, helped him walk to the car with her arm in his. She even let him drive with the radio on but his body was crouched, rigid. New commentators arrived, voices I didn't know. Geelong lost final after final. Norwood hadn't been in a grand final for ten years. He still laughed, still watched people from the doorjamb, but rather than being solitary he was simply detached. He watched us and in his face it was clear he was storing the memories, not making them.

When he grew too sick to manage without power steering, he got a new car. A little white Honda with new-car smell. Its doors thudded but didn't clunk; the windows went all the way down. It got ABC Adelaide 891, but it got FM stations, too. Sometimes we listened to music on our way into town. Sometimes a whole weekend went by without listening to the football at all.

Throughout his illness, he was still patient. He sat on the chair at the top of the steps and waited there instead. Waited for Nanna to turn off every light and check every power point. Waited for Nanna to water the plants and feed the magpies and he never ever complained.

When they took him into palliative care, Nanna was there by his bedside every moment of every day. He was still a tall man, still long-limbed and soft. She held his hands, hands that had taken him through eighty-nine years of toil and patience and his particular kind of joyful quiet.

And he waited.

And he waited, and he waited.

One Saturday night, moon high, ground damp, the football was on the radio. It was finals season, and Geelong were going tit-for-tat against Collingwood at the MCG. I was there, nose bleeding on Level 4.

Maybe they had opened the window a crack, to let that night in for him. Maybe the night sat there with him, around him – the September night, the warm football night. A nurse told Nanna she could leave if she wanted, just for a little while. To get some dinner, to breathe some fresh air, to take a break. So she did.

And while she was gone, he died.

At his funeral, my sister talked about him the way she talks about everything, with joy and exuberance. She remembered the way he put tomato sauce on everything, feeding the fish in his backyard, and how he always greeted her with a Balfour's custard tart.

But I have a different memory of him. A private, hollering, thumping memory. A season I spent in a red Datsun 120Y, learning how to love the game.

MELBOURNE: THE YEAR 2195

Angela Pippos

I take one last look at Angela before I head off into the city to face The Committee. I hold the silver-framed picture of my great-great-great-great-grandmother and stare deep into her smiling face. We share the same name and some say they can see the resemblance – the large, wide-set eyes, strong nose, powerful dark brown hair and slightly crooked front-left tooth. She looks kind. And intelligent. *Angela Pippos.* I hold the photo tightly and say a silent prayer … This is the biggest day of my life and I need all the help I can get.

I check the time again, a nervous habit. It's only halfway through the third quarter of the day, which is good. My interview with The Committee doesn't begin until the start of the fourth. Tonight I'll take the long way into town.

I board the hover tram and take one of the empty seats by a window. Sitting here gives me a chance to settle my nerves; it allows me to think and watch the world go by. As we glide silently through the quiet, statue-lined streets (it's Tuesday so there are five big games on tonight) I see tourists taking pictures of our Leaders past and present. The towering marble sculptures are scrubbed weekly, and gleam even in the fourth quarter. A group of young Japanese women giggle at the foot of one of the larger figures, one of the last Leaders to wear a suit, Gillon McLachlan. Our history tells us he was seven feet tall (and seven feet three when he blow-dried). It was shortly after his reign that the dress code laws changed and The Golden Tracksuit became mandatory attire for all Leaders. The tourists are pointing, open-mouthed, at his hair.

I reach the city and get off at Buckley Square. People are gathered in small clusters, their necks arched back, staring wide-eyed into the heavens. A laser show is in full swing. Giant beams are lighting up the night sky, paying homage to one of the former greats. A series of striking images of his changing (and pioneering) hairstyles: the perm, the mullet, the permed mullet, the surf sweep, the side-part bob. We have fifty-two Player Week celebrations a year, but I've always had a soft spot for Brereton Week. As each hairstyle illuminates the night, framing the stars in sharp fluorescent-green outlines, the great man's words of wisdom are piped down from skyscraper microphones into the streets below and hang in the air just long enough for the onlookers to catch them: 'You'd look to take somebody out, and wilfully take them out . . .'

It's a clear, cool night with only a hint of a breeze. A perfect night for footy. I head to the corner of the square to grab a quick bite at Plugger's. More piped Dermie drifts through my head: 'I drew a line in the sand . . .'

I sit at the counter and place my order. No need to look at the menu because Plugger's serves only one thing. My meat pie comes with sauce on the side. There are fourteen mounted screens, all showing tonight's games. My team, the Crows, are taking on the Devils, one of the five teams from Tasmania. The players run through the giant team hologram; an enormous black crow puffs out its chest and starts squawking, 'We're the pride of South Australia . . .' I glance over at the other screens – players, strong and steely-eyed, are running out onto grounds all over Australia. A few old-timers fist pump and nervously stroke their worn team scarves. As I near the end of my pie the Devils run through their hologram: a giant marsupial throwing three-punch combinations on a loop.

Thirty minutes till my meeting with The Committee. I leave Plugger's and walk past Melbourne's largest church, the Cathedral of Sherrin. There's a late-night service and I see it's busy tonight, full of fans of all denominations. I can hear strains of 'Up There Cazaly' coming from the choir at the front of the church and find myself humming along.

I decide to grab a jet pack from a taxi pod and fly the last leg of my journey. As I take off I gulp in large mouthfuls of crisp air. 'The kid's got talent ...' Dermott's voice is clearer up here. I blink the cold from my eyes and sail off towards the MCG, carefully navigating my way through and over the looming skyscrapers.

As I fly I find myself thinking about my foremother, Angela, again. She would be proud of my following in her footsteps. I'm sure she would. During her lifetime The AFL was only responsible for running the game. No one could have foreseen the revolution that was coming.

And it all happened pretty quickly. The competition just kept growing. Year after year after year after year. In time The AFL became the richest, most powerful organisation in Australia. Sixteen clubs soon became sixty. Marketing strategies, which had always been fairly aggressive, went through the roof. Soon The AFL owned all the television networks and radio stations, and bar a quiet, bookish and fearful minority, the public didn't seem to mind at all; they embraced it.

You would think that the controversial move to make the season last all year round – to make it endless – would have caused mayhem and madness, but remarkably, it didn't. Crime figures dropped. Match attendances and ratings grew and grew, and people, the masses, the happy masses, just seemed really content, albeit slightly zombified.

It was under the daring stewardship of The Leader Gary Ablett Jr V that the move was made to overthrow the government and install The AFL Commission in federal parliament.

The resistance shown by our political leaders was weak. Feeble, even. Both sides of the House proved to be utterly spineless. And so, after only a fourteen-hour coup the new order was established. The peaceful revolution was in place and 'The Great Blindside', as it became known, was consigned to the pages of our history books. *Long live The AFL!*

I park the jet pack and make my way to the most sacred building in Australia, The MCG, where The Committee is expecting me. I pass through the seven levels of security and stride towards the huge oak door. My hand nervously reaches for the famous sculpted knocker. I fold my fingers around the brass football boot (size 14) and rap the ancient timber with its moulded studs. The hallway echoes. *So this is it.* One last deep breath, one last silent prayer to my ancestor, and in I go.

'We've been expecting you, Angela.' The Leader nods his head. 'Welcome. Please, please … take the seat.'

There is a solitary, lonely chair placed in the middle of the room in front of an enormous curved black Italian marble desk. Seated around the desk are twelve of the most powerful men in Australia. Seven of the men are wearing dazzling silver tracksuits, four of the men are in slacks and tight, AFL-logoed, pastel-coloured polo shirts. The Leader, Edward McGuire Jr IV, sits in the middle, resplendent in a gold lamé all-in-one. It shines brighter than the silver uniforms – and, if I'm not mistaken, has tasselled arms. He has a golden whistle around his neck. They are all big men, all former players, and all have clipboards on the desk in front of them. I sit down, smiling and composed.

The Leader speaks. 'My great-great-great-great-grandfather knew your great-great-great-great-grandmother. Did you know that?' There is warmth in his small eyes and he moves his arms as he talks. (Yes, definitely tasselled.)

'Yes. She did some MC work for Collingwood.'

Without warning the men at the table burst into voice. 'God bless Collingwood, God bless the mighty Pies, go Pies, go Pies, go Pies.'

The room falls silent again and The Leader continues, his eyes slightly glazed now. 'He was a trailblazer.'

I feel I need to contribute. 'Yes. It's written in the almanacs.'

'It is, it is.' He's nodding at me approvingly. He wipes a tear from his eye. 'A great man. A visionary. As we all are here at The AFL.'

The table murmurs as one, 'Long live The AFL'.

I bow my head. The Leader continues.

'We are all about change and being progressive, inclusive, just like our forefathers. We play a role in shaping attitudes, and society; we have great power and we wield it with great care. We are proud of our work. Attendances are at a record high, and TV and radio audiences continue to break records. But what does that mean? Do we sit on our laurels? Of course we don't. We have a duty. We are duty bound. We are The AFL.'

The table again murmurs in unison, 'Long live The AFL.'

'Angela, you sit in front of the greatest minds in Australia. We are the ground-breakers and the rule-makers. We move with speed and authority. We have made a decision. The time is right. As you well know, the networks offer seventy-four channels of exclusive AFL content. All day and all night. We pride ourselves on providing the public with the best possible shows. A timeslot has opened up. It's exciting, for all of us …'

The men at the table nod their heads. They look pleased.

'We are commissioning a documentary: *A History of the Most Powerful Women in The Game*. We would like you to provide the voiceover.'

The men in the room start to clap. The clapping goes on for quite some time before The Leader blows his golden whistle and brings the room back to silence.

'That's brilliant,' I say. I'm conscious of holding my smile in place as I turn the words over in my head. *A history of the most powerful women in the game*. The sentence dissolves and I'm left with the word history. It hangs alone, gently swinging, suspended in my mind, which has gone blank.

'Yes, we have a five-minute slot to fill on Channel 48, between *Footwear of the Stars* and *Favourite Bread Recipes of Full Forwards*.'

DOULL'S GOLD

Sam Pang & Brendan Murray

I think Bruce Doull and I could be friends. I sat next to him at the last game at Princes Park. I don't know which was better: to have celebrated, first-hand, the game from the Legends' Stand, or to have crumbs blown onto me from Bruce Doull's sandwiches.

I'm slightly embarrassed to admit it, but I spent as much time watching Bruce Doull as I did the old, dark navy Blues' flogging by Melbourne. Certainly, the game itself offered little entertainment and perhaps that is why I focused on, yeah, I think I'll call him Bruce.

Bruce wore a checked shirt tucked into black jeans. He wore a pair of sneakers, not runners, and it didn't seem wrong. His beard is now gone, which is a shame, but the long, wispy grey hair attached to the back and sides of his head still flows to his shoulders. He seemed interested in the game, and I sometimes caught him looking at parts of the ground where the ball was not, parts perhaps where he once was.

Not once during the game did he applaud good play or utter a word, other than to his wife. That he did not yell encouragement came as no surprise, for this is the same man who, politely I'm sure, declined to take part in the pre-match trip down memory lane.

Bruce did not sit with old premiership teammates, drinking beer and reminiscing about glory days at Princes Park. He sat with his wife, under a crocheted blanket, pensively considering the game with a fixed pose much like Rodin's '*Le Penseur*'. In fact, the only time Bruce thawed out of his frozen state was to pour another coffee from the thermos for himself and his wife.

Bruce caught me watching him a couple of times. I tried to pretend I wasn't, but Bruce knew. I felt ashamed of invading his privacy and understood fleetingly what Brent Crosswell meant when he wrote: "Doull's game has a moral purity about it, and that is why opponents have always found it extremely difficult to be unfair to him. It would have shamed them."

I loved Bruce as a footballer. I loved him for the same reason so many Carlton fans and football aficionados loved him. He was skilful, even credited with the ability to direct his spoils. He was durable and dependable, to the point that Carlton team sheets came printed with Bruce Doull on them, and the team was picked around him. Above all, he let his football do the talking – a modesty that modern-day footballers could not understand.

Now I love him as a spectator. Bruce is gentle. He brought his own sandwiches, neatly cut into halves. He handled them delicately. The same delicacy, I imagine, he displayed when adorning his headband. Bruce is quiet. While other teammates revelled in the festivities on the field and received standing ovations returning to their seats, Bruce arrived early, politely declined interviews and discreetly departed with five minutes to play to avoid the backslapping nostalgia.

As much as I'm sure I love Bruce, I'm not sure Bruce could love me. For one thing, I enjoy a chat. I often wonder if, during his playing days, Bruce 'the recluse' actually called for the ball. Crosswell once referred to Bruce as 'a feeling' – someone with whom he aspired to converse.

I have my flaws, and I wonder if Bruce would accept me for who I am. But then again, many of his teammates had publicised flaws, too, and Bruce managed to co-exist amicably with them. With such tolerance in his heart, I feel more confident that we could be friends.

We do share some commonality. Firstly, we both shun the football world. Granted, I'm not a four-time premiership player and have not yet won a Norm Smith Medal, but I once kicked nine goals for Tongala, and have been referred to, in some quarters, as possibly the third-greatest Chinese footballer to play the game. Secondly, I prefer to watch football in relative peace and quiet. And finally, I love sandwiches, especially ones cut in halves.

I also worked in a newsagency when I was young. This bonds us, as Bruce, I'm told, owns a newsagency in Montmorency. Even at thirty-one, I would consider a paper round under the tutelage of Bruce, if he were so kind to offer.

It may be that our friendship is fanciful. Perhaps it will never have the chance to blossom. However, at the last game at Princes Park, I sat quietly beside Bruce and pretended for the afternoon that we were friends.

THE YEAR OF THE DOGS

Demet Divaroren

My parents and I arrived from the outer when I was six months old. We left Turkey for Australia, landed at Melbourne airport and settled in Footscray with all the *others.*

My *otherness* grew in the outer suburbs.

It scrunched up my face, tied my tongue. It put me in my place; a cramped space between home, where kebab smoke clouded the air every weekend, and the outside, the mainstream world that smelt of meat pies and hot dogs.

My *otherness* muddled my words. At primary school, English words hung off my tongue like baubles. They got tangled, couldn't break free from the Turkish words that were loaded with meaning. English was the language of the mainstream and my words were flimsy and transparent. I floated on the boundaries of the playground, a mute observer of the cracks on the concrete, and the green-fingered eucalyptus trees that were home to those two fat babies, Snugglepot and Cuddlepie.

I was invisible like the wind, sweeping snippets of conversation at recess and lunch, gathering clues as to where I might fit. It wasn't long before the word wog tumbled towards me.

'Are Aboriginals wogs?' a boy asked his mate one day.

'Yeah, for sure.'

'What about Chinese people?'

'Yeah, even Aussies are.'

'So anyone who isn't American is a wog,' the boy concluded.

It wasn't until the mainstream world came to our multicultural school that some understanding filtered through. Mainstream was a tall, sandy-haired footballer dressed in red, white and blue who stood in front of our class holding a football. His teammate was considerably shorter with dark curly hair but my eyes were plastered on the tall one, who looked so different to the dark and moustached Turkish heroes in the movies I watched at home. I knew two things that day: my fair-haired boy belonged to a football team called Footscray, and love was an English word that turned my heart into a tornado.

We moved to Meadow Heights when I was twelve, a suburb nestled on the outskirts of Broadmeadows in Melbourne's north. Its walking tracks were peppered with sunflower seed shells as residents exercised their mouths and feet. Shoes were left at front doors, gardens boasted tomato and cucumber patches, and the local delicatessen shelved imported pickled preserves, sheep and goat's cheese, sweet and sour jams, black olives, the staples of a Turkish kitchen. Meadow Heights was a mini Turkey that embraced and quashed all at once. It made me visible beyond our front fence where *günaydin* was the morning greeting. I belonged in this outer suburb where prophecies were seen in Turkish coffee cups and the closest thing to mainstream was the television shows that lit up our lounge rooms.

By fifteen, the space between home and school started to blur. Something inside of me was awakening. It *tap tap tapped* in history class when we discussed Gallipoli. I had a foot in each trench, and the Australian side was questioning my allegiance and my identity. That side shadowed me to Turkish School every Saturday morning, injecting English into my Turkish sentences. It wanted to be seen and heard at recess and lunch, when conversations revolved around the most pashable Backstreet Boy and which Spice Girl had the most spunk. The outer was threatening to swallow me into its dark mouth. I had to find a bridge of connection to the mainstream world.

I had to find the right words.

I made my mainstream debut in the Year of the Dogs. It was 1996. The school grounds echoed with the cheering and banter of girls gripped by AFL fever.

'Carn the Blue Boys!'

'Go the mighty Cats!'

'Come on, Dons!'

Their words had rhythm and my heart drummed to their passionate beat. I didn't know much about the game and couldn't kick a footy straight but it didn't matter. AFL entered my life with a knockout tackle, at a time when the Footscray Football Club was getting smashed on and off the field. They were the underdogs; the Scraggers, the Battlers, and I found my place among them, the team of the working class. The team that was coming of age as the Western Bulldogs. I became a Bulldog, tenacious and loyal. My one eye bulged out of my forehead and my tongue spoke mainstream.

'What a shocker!'

'You're a joke, umpire!'

'Bloody useless!'

This was a language of few syllables, where one was understood not by the number of words spoken but by their delivery.

And I delivered.

I delivered till I was blue in the face and stars exploded

in my eyes. I delivered with a guttural voice in front of the radio, at training, from the stands that chased away opposition supporters at half-time but secured my place within a Bulldog pack. I belonged in this space and learnt more than how to raise my voice. I came to understand that 'You can do it, Dogs, come on!' was more than a mantra. It represented a never-give-up belief ingrained in the Aussie culture.

A culture that shaped the other half of me.

In 1997, a ball was launched from the outer boundary line into the Bulldogs' forward fifty. Tony Liberatore picked it up, took a quick snap and the ball bulleted between the goal posts. As Libba flew into Brett Montgomery's arms to celebrate, I flew out of my seat at the MCG, trembling with excitement. It was the eleven-minute mark of the last quarter and the Doggies were now up by 28 points in the preliminary finals against Adelaide. We were off to the grand final, our first since 1961, and I had a week to turn my front yard into a red, white and blue wonderland. Except, the umpire signalled a point. His mistake severed the momentum, and the Doggies went on to lose by two points in a thriller that left us broken.

In 1998, we couldn't pick up the pieces and Adelaide smashed us in another preliminary final. Both losses knocked the confidence that I'd managed to scrape together. *You're just not good enough*, it echoed, *just like your team*. The next year, on my first day of university, I sat outside the locked room before class, fending off the voices that were trying to shove me back in my place on the boundary line. Other students sat scattered about, their conversations billowing around me.

'Yeah, me and Mum go to the footy,' a blonde-haired, blue-eyed girl said.

My ears twitched. The girl sat across from me and I caught her eye. 'Who do you barrack for?' I said, sifting through my arsenal of knowledge of all sixteen teams: the dreaded Crows, the feral Pies whose skills weren't good enough for the top eight, everyone's second team, the Saints —

'The Doggies,' she said.

'Me too!' I gathered my things and walked to where she was sitting without a second thought.

Our friendship moved from university classrooms to football grounds, where we'd unroll our handmade banners that urged our beloved team to win. 'Come on, Dogs, grant our wish, the millennium cup on a dish!'

Our words sparkled.

My language started to rhyme.

The Doggies were love, loss, spirit and belonging.

English words were no longer flimsy; they were rich with meaning.

SLEEPLESS IN SEPTEMBER

Erin Riley

I fell in love with Australian Rules football eventually, but it wasn't exactly love at first sight.

I was born and raised in Wollongong, a place where 'footy' meant rugby league and where my brothers spent their Saturday mornings playing cricket in the summer and soccer in the winter. I had barely even heard of the Victorian game. If the Sydney Swans making the 1996 grand final permeated Wollongong's regional consciousness at all, it didn't filter all the way to 6D at Oak Flats Primary School.

But then, in years to come, there were hints of its charm: in the first grand final I ever watched, with the local Australian expat group while living overseas, when I was more excited about my first meat pie in six months than I was about the game; in the story of a player, new to Australia, in the very week we returned from abroad, whose need to make a new home felt like my own; in the story of how the game evolved in paddocks in Victoria. But still, it wasn't love. It was no more than a passing interest.

Even the first time I actually went to a game, with my youngest brother and his friend in tow, I wasn't entirely enamoured. It was a one-sided contest at the atmosphere-challenged Olympic Stadium. (Or was it Telstra Stadium then? I forget.) Bored, we got up a few times to go for a walk or get food. The woman on the aisle seat yelled at us for interrupting.

But then there was a moment, not more than a week after my parents and brothers had gone away for an indefinite stint in China, and the game became my own. As the rain poured down, and Collingwood won the game, I gave my heart over to the defeated, noble Swans. Back in the car, waiting for the rain to let up enough for me to drive home, I wept. Was I crying because I'd said goodbye to my family or because the Swans had lost? I couldn't tell. But I was suddenly, consumingly, in love with the game.

And once I fell, I fell hard.

I loved the natural way the ball moved, free of arbitrary offside rules. I loved the pace and the skill of the players. I loved that a 30-point margin at three-quarter time wasn't enough to feel safe. I loved singing the song and donning the red and white. I loved the ritual and the passion. I loved the game.

My newly pressed memberships arrived in the mail ahead of the following season. I bought two: one for me, and one for whichever friend I could rope into going with me that week. I put the fixture card in my purse and planned my weekends around matches. A friend's wedding was scheduled the night we played the Bulldogs at the SCG, and so I missed my first home game since the love affair began. I snuck out between speeches to check the score in the room next door. That I can still remember the specifics of the match shows how much it burned to miss the game.

Like any new relationship, there were firsts: first time attending an away game (in Canberra), first function (an after-match, in the back of the MA Noble stand), first kick-to-kick, first friend made at the games. In SCG Bay 28 and on the Swans' message board, redandwhiteonline, I met people with whom I'd develop lasting relationships. I met fellow fans before and after matches, or for lunch. I even started babysitting the kid who sat behind me, and we'd compare notes on our tipping and, later, our dream teams.

And like all good love affairs, there was a golden period, a time when it felt that everything was perfect and would be forever. Mine was in 2005.

It was the year I made a friend who would become my football companion. Together we baked good-luck biscuits, shaped like footballs and iced in red and white, that would eventually put us on the cover of the newspaper. My days were spent studying the history of Australian football in

New South Wales, writing my honours thesis on the game. I was fully immersed.

My memories of that year, even now, are patchy and cast in a yellow hue. I'm sure there was sadness and tears and stresses, but I don't remember those. I remember sitting on the fence at the right end of the ground when Nick Davis came to save us. I remember arriving at 4 p.m. the afternoon of the preliminary final to be in line to buy grand final tickets if we won, the last year before the online ticketing system came into play. I remember not hearing the siren after Leo Barry took his mark. And I remember sitting, weeping, unable to stop the tears, when it sunk in that yes, we had won. The drought was over.

A week later, after drinking all night following the win, after the parade and the club champion dinner, I woke with the sudden realisation the season was over and I had four weeks to finish my thesis. I wasn't sure who to be in the off-season, other than a far-less-passionate cricket fan.

Sometimes I wonder if reaching the peak so early in my football life meant the comedown was inevitable. As real as the excitement and the joy was, that it came after so short an apprenticeship, after so little disappointment, meant the love had never been tested. It was an intense love, yes, but not necessarily a strong one.

Fierce love has a way of blinding you to its object's flaws, and my love of football was no different. The players were my heroes, smart and kind and athletic – unlike those NRL thugs – and the coaches brilliant leaders. Fellow Swans fans were incredible and the AFL was an organisation that managed the game brilliantly. I would not hear otherwise. Sport was an incontrovertible good, worthy of celebration and completely underappreciated by those academic snobs who thought it wasn't worth studying.

But the sadnesses of life permeated my football bubble. The end of a couple of footy friendships that didn't last the offseason, a grand final loss, a heartbreak at the hands of another Swans fan. And the greatest test of all: when footy became my job.

It seemed like the dream, the all-access pass – being paid to write about this game I adored. But the reality was long hours for little pay on the periphery of an industry that is based around men: young men on the field and older men off it. The glamour faded in light of this reality. The footballers who had been my heroes were now just the colleagues who made the lift smell.

The romance was gone. If my love of football wasn't dead, it was on life support.

So I found a new job in a field as different to football as I could imagine. I didn't renew my membership and only went to a single game that season. Footy and I were on a break.

But two days before New Year's Eve in New York City in 2009, I sat on the floor of a youth hostel with a bunch of other Australians, drinking and talking, and the subject turned to football. We talked about the teams we barracked for (Swans, Richmond, Melbourne, Geelong, Adelaide) and our favourite players. And I remembered.

I remembered the joy of sitting in the stands and screaming '*Carrrrrrn!*' I remembered the pride of watching a player stand up under pressure. I remembered the joy of feeling connected to almost 150 years of history of the game. I remembered what it was like to have this simple, uncomplicated, shared joy.

And so, in 2010, I returned to football. I became a member again. I went to away games. I made new friendships and rekindled old ones.

It wasn't the same kind of love it was before. It didn't burn as fierce inside me. But it was a sustainable one, one that wasn't my whole life, but a part of it. I wasn't Erin Riley: football fan. I was Erin Riley: writer, daughter, sister, friend, US politics scholar, football fan. Football was one of my multitudes.

This new relationship – measured and proportionate and mature – didn't blind me to football's ills the way its predecessor had. I looked on the game with fresh eyes and was sometimes disappointed by what I saw. It was a game that wasn't always kind to people who weren't what it expected.

Football made participation of those who weren't straight and white and male contingent on acquiescence: you had to accept the dominance of that group and not challenge it to belong. The choice is stark: either accept the deal or be condemned as an outsider. I chose to rock the boat, and it hasn't always been an easy choice.

And so, football and I are embarking on a new phase of our relationship, one with eyes wide open. I don't know how much longer I can keep loving a game that doesn't love me back, one that denies people who look like me a paid position on the field or behind the mic or at the CEO's desk. It constantly reminds me: *you are a visitor in this world. It does not belong to you.*

I have learnt to survive the heartbreak and disappointment. The close games lost in the dying seconds, the thrashings on the biggest stage in football. But I'm not sure how much longer I can handle the jeers and the insults and the fear.

I guess I'll find out if my love of footy is strong enough to endure this. For now, I just don't know.

OPERAMANES

Peter Rose

Yet they accuse us of being dilettantes!
A colleague interrupts my matutinal gloom
to announce that his father shared
a first-wicket partnership with mine
thirty-seven years ago during Country Week.
He even recalls the sweep that got you out,
himself scoring a century
to your costive forty-three.
(History might like to reverse this.)
Another year, serving behind the bar
at the Collingwood Social Club,
I listened to a core of die-hards
extol your prodigious torpedo punt
in the 1953 Grand Final,
the rare projectile artistry of it.
One went on to declare that

only a monumental shirtfront
stood between you and the '55 flag.
Anyone else would have sagged on a stretcher,
but not you – so the aria went.
Marvelling at my half-time rhapsodists
I mistook them for a coloratura's claqueurs,
devotees of Callas's phrasing in the
recitative leading up to 'Casta diva',
an erotic thrill in 'Ah fors'è lui'.
We are all of us clamant in the gods,
avid, hyperventilating,
worshipping with stinging hands.

IT'S A LONG WAY TO THE TOP, IF YOU WANT TO KICK A GOAL

Bev O'Connor

'If you want to go far in footy … your name has to be Beverley.' Joseph Gutnick laughed.

I laughed too. He'd decided it was time to put a woman on the board – in 1999, a highly contentious move. The first-ever female board member, joining the Essendon board in 1994, was Beverly Knight.

I was sitting in the mining magnate's luxury Kingsway offices and so far I'd found him surprisingly engaging, funny and charismatic. Eighteen months earlier he had inherited the Melbourne Football Club's presidency after a gut-wrenching battle over a proposed merger between Melbourne and Hawthorn. The bid failed, largely because Hawthorn, led by rampaging former champion Don Scott, voted against it. Melbourne, the jilted bride, was left bitterly divided.

Known for his radical right-wing politics, this Orthodox Jew had made his fortune finding gold in the Australian desert on the advice of a sage New York Lubavitcher Rebbe. He was now intent on turning the city's oldest football institution on its head.

Just seventeen years ago, women in visible footy roles were rare. Helene Bender at Geelong was the only other board member when I was elected, and of course the remarkable Jill Lindsay was an institution at the AFL, as grounds manager.

It wasn't the first time I had been targeted for a role because I was a girl. In 1993, former player and media character Peter 'Crackers' Keenan had made me the irresistible offer to be 'the token blonde' on an ABC footy panel show *Lateball.* Some women would have been insulted, but my view has always been simple: someone has to be the first and if we can do a half-decent job it should mean the barrier gates open and women can come flooding in from the outer.

I couldn't help that racing reference; fresh in my mind is Michelle Payne's fairytale win in the Melbourne Cup. The thirty-year-old became the first woman to achieve a feat most jockeys only dream of. Exhilarated from her win, her feelings came tumbling out. She thanked the trainers and owners who had stuck by her. 'I know some of the owners wanted to kick me off … I just want to say, everyone else can get stuffed, because they think women aren't strong enough but we just beat the world.' Her words were sobering. Payne had proved to the world she was as good as the best, male or female, but she couldn't have done it without the backing of the men. It's the kind of permission too many women are still waiting for.

For women a lot of resistance has been generational, from old-school men who weren't comfortable with a change to the world in which they occupied positions of power. We've had to tread carefully to ensure we take the sceptical with us and we could never have even begun the journey without being invited on it by the few men who saw the value women had to offer.

Joe Gutnick was one of those men of great contradiction I have met in my surprising football life. Many others greeted me around the highly competitive boardroom table. There's a high expectation that including a woman helps change the culture in a boardroom or in an executive leadership team. Not in my experience. Except for reining in their language, it was business as usual. If anything, I was the one who had a lot to learn about how men operate at that level – and it wasn't always pretty. Too many healthy egos that were all used to doing business their own way.

There was paranoia, backroom dealing and ultimately what some would see as betrayal. After five turbulent years Joe Gutnick sparked a boardroom battle in the middle of the 2001 season, demanding the resignation of two directors he felt were working against him. But it was his reign that ended, with a Robbie Flower–led ticket roundly defeating him in a disputed election later in the year.

It was a baptism of fire for me. In 2000 Melbourne was riding high, playing in its first grand final in twelve years. A year later we were at war again, demonstrating that the bruises of the failed merger had not healed. As much as I could I put my head down, stayed neutral and got on with doing the job I had been asked to do: reaching out to our hugely disenchanted supporter base.

Getting on with the job I'd been asked to do and the one I had the skill set for was, in hindsight, my most important learning and one that applies in all walks of life. If you want to play with the big boys and girls, you need to have faith in what you have to offer, feel confident in your skills and get on with the task, because it's not for the faint-hearted.

And so it is with footy. Although it's a game of great passions, passion alone does not win premierships and sustain clubs. But if we engage in the game where both our passion and skill lies, be it as a supporter, player, worker, or advocate, then we have a valuable contribution to make.

The Beverleys? Well, we stuck together – jointly winning the AFL Football Woman of the Year award in 2002. We were truly fortunate: we were among the first, but what genuinely excites me are all the others who have followed. Inspirational women who had to work longer, harder and smarter than the men to break through. Jennie Loughnan, who became the first football operations manager at the Kangaroos. Peta Searle, who last year joined St Kilda as a development coach after almost giving up on her dream to coach at an elite level. And Debbie Lee, a highly decorated player who has made a profound contribution to the development of the women's game and the establishment of the two current AFL women's teams.

Which brings us to the current crop: women like the astonishingly talented Daisy Pearce. She's notched up a few firsts herself. She was the number-one draft pick in the first-ever women's draft; she's won the female equivalent of the Brownlow, the Helen Lambert Medal, six times; and was one of two women to become the first-ever female presenters at the 2015 Brownlows. More importantly, I've seen her happily stand toe to toe with AFL chief Gillon McLachlan, arguing for a women's competition by 2017.

And what thrills me about that is that it's proof we finally have a generation who believe their time has come. They are kicking goals literally and figuratively, and comfortably standing on the big stage with the men, knowing they belong.

PLAY THE BALL, NOT THE MAN

Rebecca Lim

15 JULY 2015: A SUBURBAN CHINESE RESTAURANT, LUNCHTIME.

ELDERLY WHITE MAN: I want a spoon.

SMILING, CONFUSED, YOUNG CHINESE WAITRESS: (Pointing to a porcelain spoon on the table.) This *is* a spoon.

ELDERLY WHITE MAN: I want a *proper* spoon. An *Australian* spoon.

The above exchange (which I overheard while choking on my pan-fried dumpling) neatly sums up for me the whole enigma of Asian-Australians' historical relationship with AFL. It reveals entrenched notions of what constitutes a more 'proper' or more 'Australian' version of something – a spoon, say, or a footy player. The question: 'Why don't

Asians embrace AFL more?' often appears on AFL fan forums. The answer to that is complex, and has its roots way back in the 1800s.

I love the electric experience of going to a live AFL match. For me, there is *nothing* like the scale and ferocity of an AFL game: from the speed and sheer brutal physicality of the play, to the awesome niggling on the sidelines between opposing footy fans. A live match has to be one of the most visceral things you will ever experience: you're part of an actual living organism, a vast, roaring, fractious beast that is constantly biting its own tail. You may end up jumping up and down on your seat hugging the complete strangers beside you at the final siren, or find yourself wailing about life's *total lack of fairness* as you cross the overpass from the MCG. There's nothing quite like our game in the world.

But I've also always had a slightly ambivalent relationship with footy because it's never seemed – to me, at least – particularly inclusive of women, non-European ethnics, LGBTI folk or just about anyone who isn't norm (or 'Norm'). And even just *thinking* that, within the confines of the three-generation strong Carlton Football Club–mad family I married into, is enough to get me into serious trouble.

Indulge me as I try to work out *why*. Why, historically, there haven't been enough Asian-Australian players of the game, and why there continues to be an ambivalence, even a wariness, towards the game from some sections of our wider community.

As a little migrant kid in the 1970s, I grew up watching VFL footy on TV and went for Hawthorn like all my mates did. But the packs of hard-looking dudes sporting everything from handlebar moustaches, mutton-chop sideburns, shag cuts, poodle perms, mullets and surfer hair didn't remotely resemble the people I knew in real life. And the rest of Australian TV seemed to mirror the game. I can't ever recall seeing a single Asian face on the shows on high rotation at our house like *Countdown*, *Homicide*, *Here's Humphrey*, *The Aunty Jack Show*, *Cop Shop*, *Mr Squiggle*, *Skippy* and *The Paul Hogan Show*. We loved our TV. But if the telly was anything to go by, we might as well have been invisible. All the people I saw in Chinatown every week? All the Vietnamese, Indian, Sri Lankan, Malay and Indonesian people we knew? All invisible. Even when *Neighbours* finally introduced a storyline with an Asian family in the early 1990s (you read that right), they decided to deal with the matter sensitively by having a neighbourhood dog go missing and Ramsay Street in uproar because, possibly, the Chinese family *ate* it.

The magically pale backdrop of 1970s Australian television can be traced back to the longstanding tradition in Western film and TV of having white actors stand in – in 'yellowface' or 'brownface' and bad prosthetic eye makeup – for Asian characters. Mongolians, Indians, Japanese, Filipinos, Chinese, halfies: there was a perfectly appropriate non-Asian actor to fill the role like Shirley MacLaine, Anthony Quinn, Boris Karloff, Ricardo Montalban, Marlon Brando, Peter Sellers, Katharine Hepburn, John Wayne, Sir Alec Guinness and perhaps most infamously, Mickey Rooney and David Carradine (who was cast as a Shaolin monk/martial arts expert over the legendary Bruce Lee). Such 'white washing' is particularly insidious because you're unlikely to realise it's happening. The absence just *is*. Recent portrayals of Asians by actors of the calibre of Eddie Murphy (!), Christopher Walken (!!) and Emma Stone (!!!) have, quite rightly, been called into question.

If you aren't aware of the virulent anti-Chinese sentiment that led to murderous riots on the Goldfields in the nineteenth century, which fed into the push for Australian federation and the establishment of the long-enduring White Australia Policy, you weren't paying attention in History class. I'm not going to go into whether Australia is inherently more racist than anywhere else because, at some level, everyone is racist: you only have to consider the current crop of intra- and inter-ethnic wars to see that humans are a highly intolerant species. All I will say is, that as a migrant child living in towns in south-eastern Queensland and then the outer northern and eastern suburbs of Melbourne, I copped what every Asian kid of my generation copped: some variation of 'Go back where you came from', 'Ching Chong Chinaman' (applied to Chinese kids of all genders), 'slant-eyes', 'Chinese, Japanese, hope your kids turn Pekinese!' and that enduring classic, 'Do you eat flied lice?' I suspect most Asian-Australian girls of the 1970s wanted to look like Agnetha from Abba because it would have made so many problems go away.

There's been a continuous Asian presence on this continent (in a recorded capacity) for roughly 200 years: the first official Asian migrant to Australia was recorded in 1818, with special taxes and restrictions being placed on Chinese immigrants from 1855. Despite being considered 'not white enough to fight', hundreds of Asian-Australians managed to slip the restrictions of the White Australia Policy and fight in both World Wars; though it's a fact I don't recall ever being taught at school.

In a football context, there's no agreement on the exact number of players of Asian descent (including those of Chinese, Indian, Sri Lankan, Japanese, Malay, Singaporean and South Korean descent), partly because having Asian heritage wasn't something a family necessarily advertised. But from the early nineteenth century until the present day, VFL/AFL players of Asian descent number anywhere from eleven up to twenty-three players in total, depending on who you talk to. If you consider that it takes eighteen men to field a team, with up to four on the interchange bench, the entire number of Asian-Australian players in history might just make up one whole side. Raw statistics like these then feed into the whole 'Asians don't embrace/aren't "proper"/ can't play footy' stereotype.

But it's not really amazing that there has been only a handful of players of Asian descent in VFL/AFL. What's amazing is that there have been any at all. Historically, not only have Asian-Australians had to overcome the Hollywood system of casting in national life, sporting life and in the talkies, their own parents and cultural figureheads (right back to people like Confucius) have been hostile to the notion that one can make a life – moral, just, filial, wise, benevolent, whatever – from *playing a game*. It's no secret that most football players have very brief careers. It's also no secret that there are few defined pathways to parlay that brief AFL career into something that will enable a player to thrive in the bigger game of life. The number of spectacular post-AFL burnouts we get treated to by the media is evidence of that.

Moreover, if you drill down into the stats regarding known Asian-Australian players, it's clear that – in the past – there *were* entrenched notions of what constituted a more 'proper' or more 'Australian' player of the game.

The White Australia Policy was officially dismantled in 1973. Only four of the roughly twenty-three known players of Asian heritage played VFL *before* that year, and all four were of Chinese heritage (Wally Koochew for Carlton, George Tansing for Geelong, Ernie Foo for St Kilda and decorated World War I veteran Les Kew Ming for North Melbourne). For those four football clubs to buck the system and field those players at all was revolutionary for the time. Even Les Kew Ming's wife, Vera, reportedly couldn't stand to watch him play football because of the taunting from the crowd.

The story of Wally Koochew (1887–1932) – the first recorded Asian-Australian VFL footballer – throws into sharp relief many of the issues surrounding the history of Asian-Australians and our national game. Born to a Chinese father and Norwegian mother, Koochew played football for Macedon and Brunswick before being recruited by Carlton in 1908. On his selection, a Carlton member returned his ticket, alleging that by including Koochew on the team, Carlton was dealing a death blow to the White Australia Policy. After four games, Koochew was omitted from the Carlton senior side, returning to Macedon in 1909 without playing another senior game. He died in the Melbourne Hospital, Carlton, aged forty-four, his final career move involving selling hotdogs at a stand at the North Melbourne football ground. (Perhaps to be closer to his beloved game, who knows?) While we can't speculate as to why he never played again at senior level, the bare bones of Koochew's life story read like every Asian tiger mother's worst nightmare.

But despite entrenched attitudes, a thriving Chinese-Australian footballing community existed under the White Australia Policy – one of the unsung marvels of VFL/AFL history. The Chinese Goldfield League began in Ballarat on a Friday in August in 1892, when two footy teams fully manned by Chinese – 'the Miners' versus 'the Gardeners' – kicked off a longstanding Chinese-Australian Rules tradition, cheered on by a crowd of 5000 locals. This tradition went on to include Chinese-Australian footballers playing charity matches in the late nineteenth century to raise money for hospitals and other charitable causes. Games like these gave rise to the football team first fielded by the Young Chinese League in the 1930s which, until its decline in the 1980s, sought to promote greater social, cultural and sporting ties between people of Chinese descent and the wider community. (For the record, the Gardeners won the 'splendidly contested' match of 1892 by twelve points.)

The toxic social after-effects of official policy, however, perpetuated the stereotype that the Asian-Australian was a crap kick, and the fixed perspectives of the wider Asian community, and the Australian film and TV industry, certainly didn't help either. A personal case in point: when the late, great Trevor Barker came to our primary school in 1981 to give us a little coaching in drop-kicks and handballs, they used the one Asian kid in the class who couldn't drop-kick (me!) as the comedy footage at the end of the evening news story. I missed seeing it, but I was told the next day at school by all my friends that it was *hilarious* because the TV station had showed me winding up for the kick – and missing – multiple times.

Despite, or perhaps because of, my own lack of kicking ability, I encouraged my son to do Auskick and we turned up at the local oval with scores of other kids and families on freezing winter mornings just so he could get a handle on the ball and the game, and to make good on the promise of a hot hash brown after practice. He's now as rabid a Carlton-fan as his dad is. But for many migrant and first-generation Asian-Australians it's a self-perpetuating cycle: they don't see Asians playing AFL on TV so they're more likely to encourage their children to play more 'international' and 'inclusive' sports such as tennis, badminton or soccer; because the AFL can say it's multicultural as much as it likes, but it still only boasts that small, largely historical, handful of Australian-Asian players. Its multicultural program, instituted as recently as 2005, is one of the ways in which the AFL hopes to identify cultural barriers inherent in certain sections of the wider community, and seeks to make the 'many cultures, one game' tag a reality. But beyond the annual razzle-dazzle of the multicultural round, the reality is that it will take time, courage and perseverance to overcome internal resistance within community groups towards our 'strange game' (Eddie McGuire's words, not mine).

In that context, Australian-born Lin Jong of the Western Bulldogs is a genuine cause for celebration, signalling an incredibly important and *normalising* shift. Lin Jong, whose migrant father is Chinese–East Timorese and migrant mother is Taiwanese is one of the visible signs that the modern game has truly evolved and is becoming the great equaliser and 'game for all shapes and sizes' that supporters have always claimed. One day, people will just see players like Lin Jong as *footballers*, period, and the whole 'Look, there's one!' mentality will hopefully vanish.

When asked by Eddie McGuire in September 2012, 'Have you encountered racism along the way?' the rookie Lin Jong noted, 'I haven't actually. Hopefully I don't. But, yeah, it's been fine. I'm just like any other player, really.' To which McGuire replied:

> Well, so it should be and it's a great step forward. It's remarkable that in 2012 we still talk about a 'step forward' to people being treated like human beings but, as we know, it has been a progression along the way and I'm delighted that's been your experience of the game.

When Lin Jong was racially vilified by a Richmond fan in April 2015 – to the extent that police became involved – the overwhelming media response the next day was, 'What year are we living in?' Which signals that maybe it *is* getting better; for some sections of the Australian community at least.

There's nothing like seeing people who look like you, and share aspects of your cultural background and experiences, reflected and represented in your national sport. It speaks to whether your humanity is valued. I like to think that we are letting go of the notion of what a 'proper Australian' or 'proper footballer' is, and recognising that it's not what the spoon looks like that counts. It's whether it does the job.

THE ARC

Nicole Hayes

One foot, then the other, my tread heavy and slowed by middle age as I circle the oval behind my house. So different to my youth when I felt like I could fly, legs like pistons, arms like wings, shoes barely touching the ground. It's cricket season, and the nets are busy on this dry summer's day. I pound the pebbled path, eyes down, gravity jarring my knees, my ankles. My whole body wobbling and heaving where once it would sail. Ahead, a young girl is all padded up in the cricket nets, sweeping low and wide at the ball. She's ten, maybe twelve years old. I note her form, the meticulous placement of the willow, the smooth arc of her swing. The only evidence she's a girl in the swish and bob of her long ponytail and the slight curve of her pre-adolescent hips.

Two men hover over her, beside them, a young boy, around the same age, scuffing the earth with his shoe, staring at the ground, then the sky, shielding his eyes against the sun, huffing audibly.

The men speak to the girl in quiet, level voices. I am unable to follow the thread, but I pick up words like 'slice', 'long' and 'step' as I strain to hear. The girl listens, her face turned upward, focused and grave. They are coaching her, offering advice, suggestions, applauding her form, and she is taking it in, determining to do better.

The boy shakes his head, frowns up at the men. 'It's not like she's going to be a cricketer,' he says, scorn sharp in his words. He kicks at the edge of the pitch. Eyes the girl. 'It's my turn now.'

The men ignore him, train their gaze on the girl – by the slant of her nose, slope of her shoulders, the boy's sister I'd guess, perhaps even his twin. Something sharp digs at my chest and I adjust my stride. Slow to a stop. The men are talking her through her stance, adjusting her shoulders left, then right. Their voices patient and steady. 'Dad.' The boy tries again. But the father shushes his son, says to the girl's mentor, 'We can practise at home.'

I stretch my tired calf muscles, one then the other, and stand tall to open my lungs.

'It's not like she's going to be a cricketer,' the boy says again. His words like dust in the air. He gets a stern look from the father and stalks off to the other end of the net.

I want to take the girl aside and tell her to listen. To

learn. Take every chance. Seize every second. That they'll try to take it from her, this thing she loves, so she must hold tight. Tighter. And never let go.

In 1970s Melbourne, a boy born to an Anglo-Australian man would inevitably be gifted a footy as soon as he could walk, sooner in more optimistic families. My brother – my twin, and thus me by default – had to wait until our fifth birthday.

Our gifts that year were no doubt plenty – as the youngest by so many years with siblings old enough to have part-time jobs, our haul was impressive. But of them, the only one I remember is my brother's brand-new football. A Kangaroo footy for this modest family, not the costly Sherrin we all coveted.

I wanted it from the moment I saw it, which suited my brother, who needed a kicking companion to make the thing work. He would line that ball up and, even then, could kick it hard and straight – right at me. My choice was simple: mark, or stop breathing, and so I chose to mark. And mark. And mark. I got to kick too, but with less success – that took longer.

By the following winter my brother had been signed up at the Glen Waverley Rovers Under-9s. He was a good year younger than his teammates, but had more energy than his wiry frame could contain, and it was an act of mercy for the entire family when the Rovers accepted him. And because we were a one-car family, and my brother and I, in true 1970s parenting style, were 'the twins' rather than individuals, I too went along to every training session, and eventually every game, initially to watch, though that didn't last long. Too many hours spent fending off his rocket-like stab kicks, his well-aimed handballs, and the relentless tackles that ended most backyard sessions for me to stand idly by.

I don't remember the first time I joined in at training. I don't remember being asked or invited, or even asking myself. But I do remember, having ventured down to the middle of the oval in those first dark, autumnal nights where the cluster of sweaty, muddied boys huddled, hanging back, out of the way, my sneakered feet buried in the marshy grass, my eyes flicking from coach to helpful parent, awaiting the silent nod that would mean my turn.

The boys who didn't know me hated it. The boys who did, kids from school, or our street, knew that we were twins. Accepted the reality of this oddity of twos, the boy and the girl who looked nothing alike, but still, incredibly, were brother and sister. And, more impossibly, the same age. My brother's dark-brown curls, the liquid amber of his eyes, as big as saucers, and dimples that melted hearts from twenty paces. That bought him more chances at forgiveness than any single person should be entitled to. The antithesis of my straggly blonde hair, blunt, straight fringe, skin so fair my mother worried I was anaemic. We were small, though, both of us. But also unexpectedly strong. My brother, I suspect, was born with it. I, on the other hand, had developed it as a defensive measure, a way of ensuring I survived my twinhood, filled with high-stakes dares and feats of enormous agility and risk. There was no tree my brother couldn't climb. No roof he didn't attempt to jump off. The neighbourhood kids called him 'Monkey' because he could shinny up our backyard ghost gum despite its smooth, untarnished trunk – its lowest branch higher than our house – and shinny back down again without breaking a sweat. Always he would egg me on, taunt me to join him, or at least insist I remain quiet if I didn't. So I did. Over and over. A secret pact that demanded loyalty to each other beyond all others.

But footy was different. This was public. A girl playing a 'boys' sport' was unusual. And in Glen Waverley, the unusual was neither encouraged nor appreciated. But perhaps as twins we were already breaking the rules on some level. Already breaching the code. Because eventually the handful of silent objectors – their disapproving frowns, their refusal to say my name or acknowledge my very existence – faded. Or maybe they just gave up. They had their own problems, one of them the humiliation of losing to a girl.

I remember the mix of players – the boys who took to the game like starlings to flight, whose hands seemed to caress the ball when they handled it, who read the unknowable bounce of its odd shape like a story, who loved it from the start. Natural. Gifted. Devoted. Mini kings in the making, winning mentions in the local paper every week, and later – when the club appointed its first professional coach – money. A twenty here. A tenner there. Clandestine, delicious, and shocking. Distinguishing these players from the rabble in a scratchy handshake, a nod and a wink.

But there were other boys, too. Boys who hated every dirty, groping minute of the game. Who wallowed on the bench, resentful and distracted, wishing themselves anywhere but there, on those cold, wintry Melbourne Sundays, full of sweat and mud and sometimes blood. And the cries of too-deeply invested parents.

These boys struggled to get a kick, schlepped off gratefully to train with the B's, relieved not to expose their soft, uncoordinated bodies to the solid chest of a more talented teammate. Or worse, his sister.

My brother and I didn't know to be scared. We were not yet familiar with real pain, the sharp ache of a broken bone, the throb of a sprained ankle. Not the sear of jarred fingers or the rush of a concussion. We didn't consider that bone-crunching tackles or falling to the earth from the height of a shoulder could hurt like the devil. Could end, not in the glory of a free kick or a goal, but in a dash to Emergency, and an interminable wait for a doctor.

And, despite the inconvenient fact of my gender, no one spared me. Besides, it was only training; I wasn't allowed to play actual games. I'm not sure, had there been girls' footy at the time, that my parents would have encouraged me to join. Not sure that my participation was ever anything more than a quick fix for an active kid at a loose end. That I stayed, and stayed, and continued at the club throughout my primary school years, seemed entirely accidental.

I can't say my parents ever disapproved. I can't remember them complaining or warning me of the dangers. They had their hands full with four kids in general – my brother in particular. If my readiness to play kick-to-kick with him gave them a few minutes' peace, who were they to criticise? And anyway I was having a ball. I was, by then, officially a 'tomboy' – that horrible, antiquated term used to describe any girl who felt more comfortable in jeans and desert boots than dresses and pigtails. Who suffered her ballet lessons largely to ensure no one objected to the footy training on alternate nights. It felt right and good, and I loved it. The fact that footy didn't love me quite so much was just another reason to hate being a girl. Already there seemed so many – hair you had to brush, having to cross your legs when you sat, feeling like you were weaker, or lesser somehow, than your own brother.

At the start, I suspect the coach humoured me, though I'm not entirely sure why. This was after all a time when there was only one winner in pass-the-parcel, when there were A grades, and B grades, 'smart kids' and 'dumb kids' and we knew which we were – where everyone fit – from the first day we became social. Games had winners and losers, and the winner wasn't always the birthday kid, or the 'special' kid. It was whoever was the best – the fastest, the strongest, the smartest, the most agile. The kid who knew her times-tables, or his homophones. There were rules and there was competition, and if you didn't fit the mould, or rise to the challenge, you were on your own.

So the fact that I wasn't turfed out of the Rovers' training squad that first week suggests I wasn't entirely crap. That I was still playing five years later suggests I probably got better. The Rovers were good by then. Regular finals competitors, and sometime premiers. By the time we were in Grade 6, the coach had decided I was worth a game. My brother wasn't especially keen – until then he'd suffered my involvement the way we'd both learned to suffer our moniker, 'the twins'. As a collective noun, at least in the eyes of most, we were lumped together involuntarily. It happened less as we got older but I distinctly remember in Prep, when my brother got into trouble – which he so often did – and was sent to the back of the room – as he so often was – I was told to go and sit with him, in this curtained-off purgatory, ostensibly to 'make him behave'. Effectively being punished too, though I'd done nothing wrong. I remember the hot wave of shame engulfing me, and the subsequent fury – with my brother, oddly; not this appalling teacher – for causing trouble. Again.

But footy was his safe place – a place he excelled, where his energy and temper, his strength and fleet-footedness were celebrated, not stifled. Where he could pace the outer wing of the oval entirely on his hands, practise backflips in the mud, and throw his knotty, athletic body hard against the other boys' without once being reprimanded or chastened. In fact, he was applauded. He was good, my brother. Bloody good.

It's possible he saw my inclusion in the team as equivalent to our joint punishment in Prep – infuriating, but impossible to change – forced to endure the taunts from the other boys which, admittedly, faded once I started to sometimes beat them. But still. I imagine it sucked. I imagine it jarred and prickled at his growing sense of masculinity which, back then, was a thing unto itself. Footy enabled him to feel it freely, express it robustly, and make it his very own. Yet he suffered my presence on the oval, just like I did his at school, occasionally protesting to each other, but rarely, if ever, to anyone else.

My excitement at playing an actual game, however, was short-lived. The coach approached me again that Sunday, right before the game, and told me he'd tried to have the league change its rules, but they'd resisted. Had deemed me unfit to play because 'footy wasn't safe for girls'.

I did not argue. I did not protest. I didn't even cry. I just tucked that disappointment away deep inside, writing it off as another thing girls weren't allowed to do – part of a long list trumped only by the litany of things women weren't allowed to do. And as I'd done when I blamed my brother for my teacher's stupidity, I blamed my body for the world's injustice.

And so my allegiance to the game switched from that of a participant to that of an observer. If I wasn't allowed to play, I reasoned, I wasn't going to bother with the Rovers, and so I fixed my eyes on the Brown and Gold, a team I'd inherited from my mother. Endowed with the legacy of a successful footy team, and a legitimate outlet to express my passion, I spent every allowable minute of my teenage winters split between Glenferrie Oval and Princes Park, or wherever else the Hawks were playing that Saturday. In the stadium, now, no longer on the grass, stifling an urge so deep that I could pretend it wasn't there. When I finally escaped the angst of adolescence, my obsession receded to decidedly healthier levels, though I remained loyal and devout.

But, even today, there are occasions when my gut twists, deep and aching, as I watch a local game, remembering those stolen moments when I held the ball, and the ball held me. When the wind stung my cheeks and mud sucked at my runners, the Sherrin loose and beckoning, the goals begging me ever to *go forward.*

I watch the girl and her dad head for the wicket, my lungs constricted. The simple beauty of a child doing a thing she loves.

The father leans in, whispers into the girl's ear, gives her an encouraging pat on her shoulder as she steps up to the crease in the heart of the oval. Her brother delivers a shuddering fastball down the wicket, and she sweeps a wide arc toward the boundary, victory bright in her eyes.

And I move on, my feet finding a grace I thought had left me long ago, my whole body lighter because of it.

THERE WAS A CHOICE?

Catherine Deveny

Melbourne is the love of my life. But I hate football. Absolutely detest it. I've always hated it. The smell, the sound, the taste ... *Blergh*. Melbourne I would happily take a bullet for. Football, on the other hand, don't get me started. Actually I think you just did.

The only thing more suffocating than growing up marinated in something you are repelled by is having to strap on a fake smile and pretend you like it. 'Why?' I hear you ask. 'Why did you feel you had to pretend to like it? Why didn't you just say, "I hate cauliflower, I hate weeding and I hate football"?'

My twelve-year-old asked me the other day, 'Why were you a Catholic when you were young?' I thought for a minute and responded, 'Because I didn't know there was a choice.' Football was the same.

Growing up in Melbourne in the '70s and '80s, I was

embedded in a culture that was obsessed by football. I kept trying to fit in, thinking, 'Surely all these people can't be wrong, can they? What am I missing?' I decided to just pretend.

The result of faking interest in football was decades of nauseating, confusing alienation and cognitive dissonance. It was a life feeling there was something wrong with me. Footy was everywhere. Footy was everything. Who you barracked for was an integral element of who you were and said something about your personality. You could make immediate enemies or instant friends the moment you revealed your team. It was not uncommon for a son or daughter to tell their parents they were getting married and for the first question to be, 'Who do they barrack for?'

You didn't just support a club, your veins bled your team's colours. And how closely you were connected to football was a sign of your worth. 'You have a cousin in the Carlton under 19s? Well, that's impressive.'

'Front row tickets at the grand final? Grouse! Can I see the stubs?'

'Your uncle is Tommy Hafey's neighbour? Could you get his autograph for me?'

'Your dad coaches Carlton? Your dad is a dead-set legend.'

'You're married to a footballer . . .' (Stutters and staggers into a speechless heap.)

Footballers were – and I am not putting too fine a point on it – gods. Back then, footy was the only way bogans could get famous. These days we have reality shows.

Everywhere you looked there were bumper stickers: 'One Eyed Pies Supporter!' 'Died in the Wool Demons Fan!' 'Go Bombers!' 'EON FM Rocks the Bulldogs!' Have the times changed, or have I just moved suburbs?

Come to think of it, not only did football dominate the conversation and commentary of my first twenty years, it even inveigled itself into fashion, décor and pop music. The barbershop quartet team anthems with the jaunty brass backing were hideous enough but the schmaltzy formulaic pop songs were the real shockers; 'One Day In September', 'Aussie Rules I Thank You For The Best Years Of Our Lives', 'The Thing About Football' and, of course, 'Up There Cazaly'.

The cloying lyrics and emotionally manipulative music would invoke involuntary goosebumps, teary eyes and a subsequent feeling of embarrassment. The rousing chord progressions, choirs in full flight, strings in octaves and timpani created a confected majesty that tapped into our animal brains. We're not that smart. Do keep in mind we're all just monkeys wearing clothes.

The ubiquity of football was even more amplified because of where I lived – in the housing commission area of Reservoir. Reservoir was a working class Mecca where the worst thing you could be accused of was being up yourself. Football was considered a great leveler, an arena where even the dumbest could find some fame, some kudos, some respect. Football was the only game in town. You chose a team and you stuck to it. It was almost like choosing your star sign. And it was for life. You couldn't change. My childhood was infested with footy-branded beanies, scarves, show bags, stickers, duffle coats, badges, bath towels and doona covers. In: group loyalty. Out: group hostility.

Footy cards were big. Kids would run through four lanes of traffic to grab an empty aluminium can they spotted on the side of the road so they could trade it in for a few cents. They would save up their 'can money' so they could go up to the milk bar to buy a packet of footy cards. A packet consisted of five cards with pictures of players on one side and their 'stats' on the back, with a stale stick of chewing gum shoved in for good measure. Kids, mostly boys, would sit around at playtime trading cards. 'Got him, got him, need him, got him, swap ya, got him, got him, need him, got him'. Their dream was to 'collect the set'. I never knew of anyone who did.

Back then, I barracked for North Melbourne. Why? Well, why does anyone barrack for anyone? I barracked for North Melbourne because my mum did and I was a suck. I had no idea where North Melbourne was, wasn't keen on blue and white, and had no interest in kangaroos. But at least I had a team. As I navigated my childhood and found myself embedded in constant football I could at least feel a part of one of the twelve tribes that made up what appeared to me at the time to be the world.

'So who do you barrack for, young Cathy?'

'North Melbourne.'

'Ah, never mind, I won't hold that against you.'

What does that even mean?

Football was all anyone talked about. I would see people listening to it on the radio, watching it on the television, and as spectators at the footy. These grumpy, surly, disappointed people were alight with excitement at the game. The game! The game! The game! Yet many of us thought, 'Who cares who gets the ball and who passes to who and who kicks the most balls and who scores the highest and who's on top of the ladder and who gets the wooden spoon?' But we dared not utter a sound lest we expose that we were 'up ourselves' or 'unAustralian'.

There was a book that came out in 2002 called *Sheilas, Wogs and Poofters*. It was about the history of soccer in Australia but the title perfectly illustrates what people thought of you if you didn't follow footy. You were either a sheila, a wog or a poofter. You were an outsider and not to be trusted.

I know most people see football and think, 'Community! Team spirit!' They look at footballers and think, 'Athletes!' I look at some of them and just think, 'Rapists in shorts.'

People keep telling me football's improved on the misogyny, homophobia and racism front. I'm not convinced. Football only progresses when it has to. When it would be bad for business. The AFL are never pioneering in policies advancing women, LGBTIQ, multiculturalism or people with disabilities. Unless it means they'll lose shareholders.

I have three sons. All in high school. None of them are into football at all. We didn't discourage them. To the contrary. We made sure there were balls around that they could play with and if they showed any interest we bought the appropriate colour jumper, went to grand final barbeques and even organised for one of the boys to see a game at the MCG. I have a vague recollection of one of them spending a couple of mornings at Auskick. I think he only went because he heard there were sausages.

The reason we did not actively discourage our sons' interest in football was simple. While their dad is not into football either, he would tell me about the importance of being able to chat about what's going on in the world of football in order to lubricate social and work situations. It's easier than having to explain yourself with people you were probably never going to see again, or people you just had to work with.

When the boys were young there wasn't a function, party, get-together or barbeque without a boozy older man bailing them up with, 'So who do you barrack for, little fella?' To which they would reply, 'No one.' It would take a while to register and the old bloke would look startled, hurt and a bit angry. Then he'd say, 'You have to barrack for someone.' And they would respond with something like, 'Why?', 'No you don't,' or 'What difference does it make?'

At a recent dinner party I met a woman who was into football and I asked her if she could guess who people barracked for. She was pretty confident she could. So we halted the chat about renovations, schools and medical dramas and the woman guessed which teams people around the table barracked for. Despite not knowing much about them, she mostly got their teams right.

People occasionally question the video games or movies I let my sons watch. When I respond I would much prefer them play computer games than watch or participate in football, they are gobsmacked. At least computer games come with a rating system, warning of confronting or potentially offensive content. Video games are constantly under attack for their supposed 'bad influences'. Of course, not everything about them is brilliant. As my old Iraqi mate says to me, 'Every house has a toilet.' But people are constantly criticising them, hand-wringing about 'all that violence', yet have no problem with football.

I rarely have any contact with football now. Which is liberating. And a relief. It seems far less pervasive than it was when I was young but occasionally I find myself unable to escape it in conversation, on the radio or blaring on a screen. 'Men, men, men,' I say in my head as football infects the space. If my sons are there, I say it aloud.

'Oh look! Something different! Let's cut to some men commentating with other men about what some men did. Time to show a bit of respect as an old man is being driven around the MCG in an open-top car and the men commentating are calling him a hero and a legend and people are clapping and crying. Back to the men talking about what the other men are doing. Now for a commercial break. Men drinking beer, men tending the barbeque, men driving cars while women sit in the passenger seat. Oh, here's a woman! What is she saying? "Being a mum is the most important job in the world." And what's this ad for? Toilet cleaner. Now back to the football. Men, men, men, men, men.'

BEATING THE JINX

Sophie Cunningham

In the early '70s Dad regularly took my brother and me to watch Carlton play at Princes Park. My brother, Saul, who was only five or so, was put in a baby's car seat and strapped high up on the wire fence at the back of the outer so he could see over all the heads of the taller blokes. Dad used to go to the game with a group that included the playwright Jack Hibberd and other Pram Factory identities. As far as they were concerned, the outer at Princes Park was a sacred site. It was a very male tradition and as a child I came to resent the fact the game bonded my father and brother in a way that excluded me. Even when I was only eight years old, I found watching lots of blokes get pissed before, during, and after the game pretty intimidating.

When Saul was slightly older, my great-uncle attempted to lure him to Hawthorn by giving him the team's jumper and scarf. I was not offered such trinkets. My great-uncle's attempts to get my brother to change teams were viewed as sacrilege. My decision to stop barracking for Carlton when I was a teenager considered even worse. More shockingly still, I took up barracking again ten years later *for another team.*

The team was called Geelong and while I did not go out for long with the man I'd crossed over for, I did stick to Geelong, a team that is, as Tim Lane noted when reviewing John Harms' book, *Loose Men Everywhere*, 'a metaphor for life. They excite, they depress; they build up hopes, they fail to deliver; perhaps more than any other, they're the team of laughter and tears.'[1] It was also a bit like falling for the depressive bloke who tells good jokes at parties but always leaves early and alone. This was especially the case when I began to barrack for them in the early '90s. Geelong had a painful association with loss that became more acute after its horrendous run from 1989 to 1995, when, despite the presence of Gary Ablett Senior, they lost four grand finals. The worst of these was their battering by the West Coast Eagles in 1994, when Geelong scored 8.15 (63) to the Eagles' 20.23 (143). Writer John Harms became so attached to the club's failure that he was forced back in 1995 to wonder how he would cope if Geelong did win at the end of the season. It was twelve years more before he was tested on this front.

While those dry years haunted the club's supporters, midfielder Jimmy Bartel pointed out during an interview before the 2007 grand final that none of Geelong's current players were in the team during those long and terrible years. Despite Bartel's protestations, this sense of being jinxed took a long time to shake – notwithstanding the team's extraordinary success over a decade. This success did, of course, lead to a profound reassessment of the Geelong persona. That depressed guy at the party had become the life of it, dancing around the living room shaking maracas, the last to leave. John Harms seemed to recover from the fear that he wouldn't cope with a world in which Geelong were victorious.

If barracking for Geelong in the early '90s was a stressful affair, from 2007 to 2011 it was glorious. A particularly memorable game in those years was the preliminary final in 2007, a night match held at the MCG. The game was between Geelong and Collingwood and was extremely close. There was only a minute to go and Geelong was winning by 12 points when Paul Medhurst kicked a goal for Collingwood. The exchange between Triple M's commentators captured, in that inarticulate but passionate way that only footy commentary can, the drama of the occasion.

'It's a goal, bloody hell.'

'Bloody hell, Jim.'

Geelong held on for the vital few seconds after that and won the game by only five points. What was on the mind of Geelong supporters at that moment was, of course, the jinx. The fear that Geelong did not know how to win. With another goal to Collingwood, Geelong would, once again, have been coodabeens.

Football does this: captures something about the absurdity of life, the tricky combination of hard work and luck, which reduces barrackers to a kind of superstitious fatalism. A game can turn, and a club's history can revolve on small moments of courage, some intelligent coaching, and on things as ephemeral as the weather, the state of a player's, or indeed, the coach's marriage. There was much gossip and speculation that Geelong's expected rise to the top of the league did not occur in 2006 because coach Mark 'Bomber' Thompson had personal problems.

After that win against Collingwood in the preliminary final I was so desperate to see Geelong win their first grand final in forty-four years that I finally got a ticket by asking people I worked with to source me one – a task well outside their job descriptions. I paid $600 to sit in the very back row of the MCG. It was worth it even though I, like the nervous fans Matthew Klugman interviewed on the subject, could barely bring myself to believe that victory was ours:

> Fresh memories of deceptive expectations can even lead barrackers to extreme denials of hope. In 2007 some Geelong followers provided an absurd example of this after the team almost lost the preliminary final they had expected to

> dominate. Though Geelong led Port Adelaide by more than 60 points in the third quarter of the ensuing grand final, some Cats fans still refused to believe that the long-awaited victory was finally theirs.[2]

I only relaxed at the point in the fourth quarter when it became clear that even if Port kicked a goal a minute they could not win. Geelong went on to beat Port Adelaide by a record margin (for a grand final) of 119 points.

Let me leap forward from 2007 to 2009. Geelong was playing St Kilda on a Sunday in July at Docklands Stadium. It was Round 14 and neither Geelong nor St Kilda had lost a game up to that point, though Geelong had come close a couple of times. Geelong's loss to Hawthorn in the 2008 grand final had been shattering, and Geelong had been trying to regain its composure ever since. They were looking like a top team on the way down; St Kilda, a fresh team on the way up. At the beginning of the game, as the Saints snapped three or four quick goals, it looked as if Geelong would be slaughtered, but then, slowly and painfully, they began to crawl back. The tension was such that I was almost physically ill. When Cameron Mooney kicked a goal to bring Geelong to within two goals of the Saints, I put my head in my hands and stopped watching. When Geelong ended up losing by six points, I sobbed. If that all sounds a bit much, let me quote Melbourne writer and Essendon supporter Tim Richards on the subject of barracking:

> We tie our own emotional wellbeing to the triumph or failure of a group of young men engaged in an ostensibly meaningless pursuit, probably because we know at heart that the whole of existence is absurd, and that the meanings we construct and share make as much sense as anything else . . . We football fans need to imagine that the number 5 in our colours has our emotional wellbeing in mind as he lines up the goals. That he cares about us as much as he cares about himself.[3]

Shortly before the 2009 grand final, Cameron Mooney was interviewed about the pressures and exhaustion that come with dominating the game over so many seasons. Football is harder than it used to be. Players are expected to play up to twenty-six games in a season, including finals – in addition to perhaps four preseason matches. They have to travel interstate to games, and in 2009 Geelong travelled interstate five times, including two trips to Perth. Not surprising then, that they began to be dogged by injuries. Top ruckman Brad Ottens was injured in Round 2 and didn't play again in the seniors until Round 22, just before the finals. For the Round 15 match against Brisbane, following the loss to St Kilda, star players Steve Johnson, Gary Ablett Junior and Matthew Scarlett were out of the Geelong side with injuries. Johnson had a hip injury and barely played a match until the preliminary final against Collingwood. The psychological wear and tear began to show. Mooney was haunted by a couple of shocking missed goals in the 2008 grand final, and finally sought out a sports psychologist who helped him regain his confidence. Mooney's – we like to call him Moons – return to form was a significant confidence booster for his teammates: his sensitivities somehow reflected the team's. He was, if you like, a weathervane.

In the 2009 grand final Geelong were playing St Kilda once again. Predictably, after three years of determined dominance, they were no longer the underdogs. This time it was St Kilda that had been waiting more than forty years to win a premiership.

My wife, Virginia, is a passionate Cats fan (of course) and we were lucky enough to get tickets to the final, for a third year in a row. What is clearest in my memory of each year is the half-hour walk from our house to the MCG. In 2007 it felt momentous though we had hope in our hearts. In 2008 we were nervous and Geelong was, indeed, humiliated. This year, 2009, was different again.

As we walked through Fitzroy Gardens in the hail on that cold bleak day, it seemed more important than ever that Geelong win, but, given the team's exhaustion, it was no certainty they would. I'd even received a blessing from my Carlton-barracking father. 'I hope you win,' he'd offered, a statement that no doubt cost him. As well, both Virginia and I had too much understanding of the way history works.

We knew that if the club lost two out of three grand finals they would not be remembered as the team that was dominant through the second half of the decade – they would be the guys who were almost the best in the league but never quite had what it took.

The first quarter looked bad for the Cats. The rain kept coming down and we all huddled in beanies and coats, clapping our hands together to keep warm – an extraordinary contrast to the year before when we'd got sunburnt and people in the crowd had collapsed from heat exhaustion. In the second and third quarters the game evened out. It became tough; dirty and akin to hand-to-hand combat. It was hard to pick the difference between the teams. At the beginning of the final quarter St Kilda were winning by seven points but a few minutes in, Geelong's Tom Hawkins landed a goal. While it was fifteen minutes before another goal was kicked, the battle for possession of the ball was so intense the game was as gripping a quarter of footy as I've ever seen. 'The Saints' defence are like men crazed,' said one commentator. There was a misty rain falling and the ground was muddy. The times when Gary Ablett Junior got the ball were, as always, extraordinary – he seemed to fly out of the pack of an ordinary game and transform it into something else. With only six minutes to go, when Geelong was two points behind, a string of passes between Cory, Byrnes, Mooney, Chapman and Rooke resulted in Rooke kicking the ball through the posts. St Kilda's Stephen Barker flung himself at the ground, slid along it until his head slammed into the post and touched the ball, reducing a possible six points to just one. The score was now to 67 to 66.

Meanwhile, in what seemed increasingly like a symbol for the tenor of the game, St Kilda's Brendon Goddard, his broken nose strapped to his face with gaffer tape, charged around the ground like a wounded bull. The game moved into time-on. Geelong's Steve Johnson had had a shocking day, but he spotted Ablett out alone and kicked towards him. Zac Dawson desperately smothered it, but Matthew Scarlett's inspired toe-poke off the ground put the ball into Ablett's hands. The rest is history. Ablett held on tight and raced down the ground, shepherded by Scarlett, then kicked the ball 80 metres. Scarlett is, to my mind, the kind of player who makes Geelong. Always playing defence, he doesn't get the flashy play – but victories often turn on his ability to control the ball. At this moment he had a look on his face that said, 'I will die before I let us lose this game.' Travis Varcoe handballed to Paul Chapman, who snapped up his third goal of the game. The scores were now 67 to 72.

There were about four minutes to go and Geelong was soaking up the seconds. Geelong supporters held their collective breath. A few seconds later, young defender Harry Taylor (who, with his lanky body and old-fashioned looks, appeared to be in a match circa 1940) marked the kick-in and the next thing I knew Rooke was in the goal square and had marked the ball. The siren went. When I watched the replay I saw that the camera wasn't even on him when he kicked the goal – the first goal ever to be kicked in a final after the siren. Instead there was a shot of Bomber Thompson leaping onto his desk, Chapman leaping into the air, Mooney running down the ground and various Geelong players rolling around on the ground together. Cameron Ling (who went on to be appointed captain when Tom Harley retired a few weeks later) had a microphone shoved in his face and said the game had been 'about individuals not superstars, about team effort'. Young Matthew Stokes (left out of the final team after playing in the 2007 and 2008 finals) strode onto the ground to hug Ling, trying not to look devastated about his exclusion from the team.

In contrast, St Kilda's captain, Nick Riewoldt, looked stony-faced, and Brendon Goddard was a broken man. St Kilda had only been beaten twice the entire year, by a total of seven points. They'd been as desperate to win as Geelong had been in 2007. It was heartbreaking, as well as exciting. I cried so much that an irritated St Kilda fan turned to me and said, 'You fucking won, love.' Indeed.

As we walked back through Fitzroy Gardens I announced to Virginia and her family that now that Geelong had learned to win, I could let go of the need to keep winning. I was still, at heart, one of those '90s-era Geelong depressives, unable to hope too hard. But I had one more joyous lesson to learn, though it was not, for a year or so, obvious it would be there for the learning.

Max Rooke retired at the end of 2010. At the beginning of 2011 Gary Ablett Jnr moved to the Gold Coast Suns and Tom Harley retired. There was an acrimonious fall out with coach Bomber Thompson, while Chris Scott, the new coach, was relatively inexperienced. But good things were happening too. Without star power to fall back on the team worked together more tightly. While the boys were all looking older and moved more slowly, their experience was more than compensating. In 2011 James Podsiadly, who'd joined the team in 2009 at the age of twenty-eight – pretty ancient by football standards – had kicked 52 goals and averaged over twelve disposals per game. For all these reasons Geelong, once again, found themselves in a grand final, this time against the reigning premiers, Collingwood.

Cameron Ling really came into his own as captain, and held everything together. Tom Hawkins, a young player, kicked three crucial goals and took nine marks. Podsiadly injured his shoulder and had to be taken off in the second quarter but Steve Johnson, who'd injured his knee in the preliminary final and spent most of the week in a hyperbaric chamber, kicked four goals. Jimmy Bartel kicked three goals from half forward, one of which he had to curve around from deep along the sideline. Even more impressively still he had 28 possessions. For the first part of the third quarter, it was goal for goal, with the lead changing five times. In the thirty-first minute, Tom Hawkins kicked his third goal of the game and Geelong now led by seven points.

The sun was high and bright. Mature players, no longer at the top of their form physically, played smart and hard and suddenly it was clear to me: we were about to experience the sweet pleasure of beating Collingwood in a grand final. There wasn't the anxiety of previous years; no tears, just joy. In the end Geelong won by 38 points, 18.11 (119) to 12.9 (81). When Chris Scott joined his men on the ground after the win he was effusive and emotional. It was beautiful to behold.

And so we entered the years of letting go: Cameron Ling announced his retirement a few weeks after that final, as did Brad Ottens. Matthew Scarlett retired in 2012 and Joel Corey at the end of 2013. Josh Hunt was delisted and went to Greater Western Sydney. James Podsiadly went to Adelaide for a bit before retiring while Paul Chapman moved to Essendon. Travis Varcoe now plays for Collingwood. Matthew Stokes and James Kelly played their last game in 2015, which was also the first year in nine that Geelong didn't make the finals. Distressingly, Steve Johnson was not offered a new contract and is off to Greater Western Sydney for 2016. Tommy Hawkins, Corey Enright, Tom Lonergan, Harry Taylor and Jimmy Bartel are now the only members of that era: leaders in a once-again youthful team. But something happened in those golden years of the early twenty-first century. Geelong won three premierships in five years, transforming themselves into the best team of a decade. They learned how to win. And neither the team nor their fans will be forgetting that any time soon.

---

1. 'Australian Rules for Commitment', Tim Lane, *The Age*, 22 July 2002.
2. 'Footy: The Season of Love, Faith and Agony' by Matthew Klugman, *Meanjin* 68:3, p. 70.
3. Email from Tim Richards to Sophie Cunningham, 29 January 2010.

1991

Alicia Sometimes

When Chris Langford was king. When the MCG needed some time to heal so the grand final moved to Waverley. When you could climb the steep, uneven hills at its entrance and listen to the rising caterwaul of the crowd. When you couldn't afford a ticket to the big game so you rested outside the members' stand with a flask of warm tea, a transistor and your sauce-stained Record. When you could hear the euphonious sound of 'Go Hawks' build before the siren. Where the voice of Angry Anderson caterpillared its way through the walls and hugged you uncomfortably like tight earmuffs. Where you couldn't see the azure Batmobile until the replay the next day but knew instinctively something was culturally amiss.

When Tuck was clean-shaven. When Ayres was full of ubiquity and mullet. When the younger Hudson was blond and dynamic. When Dunstall would lean into each mark before the ball was even kicked. When Collins would chip away slowly down the wing. When Platten's baulks were all ballet. When every drop punt would land between the posts with a hopeful thud. When Dear was the height of acuity and his snaps for goal rippled visibly into the seats of those in front.

When fans mocked goal umpires by running onto the ground and miming their decisions. Where pre-match toilet paper would rain down instead of confetti. When you knew the light and wind at Waverley was just a little slower and colder than everywhere else. When full-forward meant chasing 100 goals a season. When you still wore a duffle coat but the sleeves stopped at your elbows. When you added pink and purple to your brown and gold. Where you looked ahead at the car park and knew, off-season, this was where you would learn to drive your Datsun 200B.

When you'd seen Condon train at Glenferrie and knew he'd deliver. When you heard on the radio that Tuck passed to Mew who packaged it all up for Dunstall. When he kicked that goal and you started screaming. When you knew Brereton was full of strut but could always follow through. When you thought he was the one being singled out just for being a genius. Before you heard years later he had racially taunted Chris Lewis and you felt floored and sickened. Back when you raised your arms in the air ripping your coat because Dermie had kicked four. When you kissed the air because this felt like a September honeymoon.

When Langford gave Sumich two 50 metres and you thought that was it. When Mainwaring, Lewis, Pyke and Matera began to thunder and you bit your nails. When the mantra in the press had been 'Too Old, Too Slow' and you thought West Coast might be too powerful. When their year was courageous, towering and earmarked for history. Later fans would forget that we even played here. When the term 'Arctic Park' had been used as late as August. When you hadn't made it in 1990 but thought it was a one-off. When 1991 felt like an open bracket not a closed one. When you braced yourself for the last quarter.

When you heard the final siren and you fell completely apart. When your cheers felt italicised. When roads were weaving and congested leaving the ground. When you lived so close you could walk home. When you skipped a little too much and it felt like hubris. When you waved your flag above your head at all the raucous cars. When you thought the best days were ahead of you. When it felt too nostalgic to look back. Where you tried to catch yourself before you walked back in the door. Where you composed yourself for a moment before deciding the win could breathe directly into you. And you waited seventeen years to shout so openly again.

The Game

EMMA
Oh God. Here we go...

KATE
So tense

NICOLE
I can't see the game – updates please!

EMMA
That's bullshit

NICOLE
What's bullshit?

LUCY
Worst decision ever.

NICOLE
Score?

EMMA
They're up by 6. Hang on…

NICOLE
HANG ON FOR WHAT???

EMMA
12. They're up by 12.

NICOLE
Crap.

KATE
Actual score: Them 27 Umpires 15.

ALICIA
Genuine question: Can one ever pay too much for Hawthorn memorabilia? Asking for a friend.

THE BLAZER

Van Badham

The most beautiful photograph I have of my mother is one taken at the saddest time in both of our lives.

Two years ago my father, John, who was my closest friend as well as the love of my mother's life, died of lung cancer in Sydney's Calvary Hospital. My mother and I held him as he took his last breath. We allowed the nuns to lay him out for us. We clasped one another's hands as we looked at him for the last time and, amid floods of tears, we returned to my mother's now half-empty house and settled into an indefinite period of mourning.

I can't remember much about the days that followed – only that we somehow managed to organise a funeral service and perform what rituals of farewell our wet eyes and weak limbs allowed us, and that relatives and friends cleaned the house, cooked our food and poured many, many cups of tea. The days passed in a colourless blur – my mother erupting into the sudden, angry tears of resentful widowhood, me curling into the corners of the couch with a quieter but equal grief. Neither of us left the house, not having the energy to do so, or the will. If asked to remember the weather of those weeks, I'd tell you it was heavy and grey, although it probably wasn't. The first day of any sunshine I remember was the day my mother suggested she might get out of the house 'for a bit', go around to her friend Julie's, and watch the Swans game on TV.

I urged my mother's adventure, and once she committed to go she attired herself with due sporting reverence: a white shirt, red trousers, red cap, red scarf and the first smile she'd worn without tears since Dad died. I hurriedly snapped that photo, because here was the first glimpse of life to be led outside the house of our sadness. Meaning and purpose could be found again, and, for my 72-year-old mother, this meaning and purpose was in the community of fandom and her love of the Sydney Swans.

My father used to joke that his and Mum's was a mixed marriage, given he'd been a season-ticket holder for the NRL's Roosters before his legs got bad, while she was a light-in-the-eyes zealot for the AFL. Fortunately, there was no rivalry – 'the great game' in our household was defined by whatever happened to be on TV at the time. Dad's last indulgence for himself was the purchase of a plasma as big as a wall with an anything-with-a-ball satellite TV subscription to go with it. My parents kept themselves as sleepless with international rugby union tournaments, cricket, tennis or soccer's World Cup as they did in full vocal health screaming encouragement at the Roosters or the Swans onward from their personal lounge room stadium. Only occasionally did a programming clash of a Swans game versus a Roosters one provoke division between an otherwise united pair. In the infrequent Battles of the Birds, my father always managed to retain possession of the TV remote, but my mother pointedly listened to the game's broadcast on the radio – before becoming friends with Julie and going over to her place.

I think Mum's defiant devotion to her Swans was a source of admiration in my father. His own ambition to become a professional footballer was devastated by an injury, but he lived his post-playing life around the industry, and governed himself by codes of team loyalty, dedication and pride that anyone could see also governed her. How else to explain her fervour for a team like Sydney, who endured so many decades without a premiership?

It began, she tells me, with her childhood fascination with an extraordinary cream and red blazer that hung in the wardrobe of her bachelor uncle, Neil. Neil was one of five children belonging to Thomas Bowler, who emigrated from Ireland penniless and, upon arriving in Australia, more or less remained so. Before my mother was born, Neil had apprenticed as a printer in Sydney and during the Depression he'd found some work in Melbourne. Perhaps more to establish some friendly connections rather than through any great love of the game, Neil got himself involved in some Australian Rules kickabouts with the lads of his new locale. Lean and tall in the way the rugby league players back home in New South Wales weren't, Neil found himself suited to the leaps and speed and aerialism of his new code, and immersed himself in it. Thomas Bowler's family was soon informed that Neil was pursuing a professional career in the strange southern sport; he'd been recruited to a club.

My mother can't remember which club it was, what league status or where; poor luck struck Neil too soon for the family to absorb many of the details. Just before his team played their league final Neil was in a car accident that pulverised his arm. He remained in hospital while his team went on to win the game. His consolation at their victory was diminished when he learned that on the club's prize night every single player had been awarded a victory blazer except for him, although he'd played with them every other game, all season.

Neil's teammates raised money among themselves to purchase a victory blazer for their wounded friend. It became his proudest possession and, Mum said, a symbol of perhaps the greatest kindness Neil would know. 'You didn't get a chance to own many nice things during the Depression,' she explained to me. 'It really was a wondrous item – exotic, among the kind of poverty they lived in. And with the story attached to it, of Melbourne and this different kind of football we didn't really know anything about, it fascinated us.'

'Us' was the gaggle of Thomas Bowler's grandchildren, eight in all. Their mothers, Neil's sisters, took turns looking after them while holding down jobs and – in my grandmother's case – sending a husband off to the Second World War. Neil returned to Sydney after his accident, unfit for war service, and aided the clan where he could. My mother and her cousin Sharon, the oldest girls, idolised Uncle Neil, hung off his arms, admired his blazer, begged for more of his stories. When highlights of the then VFL began to be broadcast on New South Wales television, this romantic memory of Australian Rules, and the community that bought my mother's broken uncle his blazer, re-inspired my mother's interest in the foreign sport. I was a small child in the 1970s, but I remember Uncle Neil at my grandmother's, watching the VFL on TV, explaining to my mother what a mark was, while cousins and others called the game 'aerial ping pong' and denigrated the players for an absence of sleeves.

But by the 1980s, my mother certainly knew what a mark was, and the raw team she picked to support was learning it, too. Mum chose the Swans as her team because

'I'm from Sydney, Van – ridiculous question!' and by the centre of that decade Geoffrey Edelsten's purchase of the team had thrust them into a spotlight. Perhaps not glamorous, but at the least glitzy. Edelsten's notorious taste in cars, gilt, grand pianos and girls had aroused an associative curiosity about his team. Sydney crowds were finally attending their own team's games, and Edelsten was rewarding them with dancing girls, a 'Sock it to 'Em, Sydney' theme song, confetti, balloons and the Swans star player, Warwick Capper. With blond Cleopatra locks and famous white boots, Capper was not only the one Aussie Rules player Sydneysiders could at least recognise, he was also the perfect on-field representative for Edelsten's ostentation – with the added attraction of tangible footballing talent. Sydney loves a winner, and with the Swans now winning home games, it didn't take much persuading from Mum for Dad to drive us out to the SCG to see them play. Dad was curious to see Capper, too. With an atmosphere that was half sport, half Vegas show, it was unsurprising that Mum and Dad were running into increasing numbers of their friends when we got out to the ground.

Mum was also making friends because of her detailed understanding of the team and the game. At her job in the public service, she discovered a shared passion for Swans-themed footballery with co-workers as eager as she was to embrace Victorian-style fandom. By the 1990s, Mum was building shrines at work to pray for the recovery of player Tony 'Plugger' Lockett from a groin injury, introducing a novel 'colour in Plugger's groin' participatory element with textas supplied for communal devotion. As Dad's health worsened and he limited himself to living room sports and the plasma, Mum was finding eager replacement companions for the Swans home games. By then, Edelsten was gone and the team left behind was talented and pushing ever closer towards the legitimacy of a finals run. 'It was when Plugger was playing that I think it got crazy for me,' my mother says. 'Because now we had an actual chance of winning.'

Sharing hope in that chance were my mother's new friends, Carol and Julie, two local women she met on the bus home from work. 'Julie's the one you should talk to about the footy, not me,' said my mother when I told her I was writing this. 'She knows all about the games and the players. She keeps a diary.' For her part, Julie was overjoyed to discover a local aficionado of what is still, to too many, a foreign game. Julie and Mum became regular game companions, and when I was overseas, my left-behind boyfriend joined them, too. From this they developed their own exclusive sub-fandom and nomenclature. They nicknamed a particularly youthful-faced player 'Babyface', which they quickly shortened to 'Baby'. '*Carn, Baby!*' they howled during one game, only for a kid of maybe eleven to turn around in front of their seats and ask the crowing old girls, 'Who the fuck is Baby?' It's this camaraderie that I think Mum realised she needed when she took those first tentative red and white steps out of the house after Dad died, and she's kept taking them ever since. If she can't make it out of the house for whatever reason, she and Julie watch the game from their homes and phone one another to exchange commentary. She's disappointed when they lose, of course, but fortunately the disappointment never lasts longer than a slightly downbeat phone call to me with a recount of game highlights.

It's fortunate that as Mum's emotional investment in the game has grown, so has the performance of the team. The year the Sydney Swans won the premiership for the first time, she travelled into Sydney's CBD for their celebration parade, popping into her cousin Sharon's workplace on the way as an act of family commemoration. 'Because we'd both started this when we were kids with Uncle Neil, I felt I needed to see her and make that connection,' Mum says. 'And I was lucky I did because she knew it was going to be busy. I said, Come off it, Sharon, this isn't Melbourne, there'll be a few out but not that many, and she said, Barb, it's not a Melbourne game anymore. Half an hour later, I was up the front and the crowd was six deep behind me.' Mum was staggered. 'I couldn't believe it!' she says. 'And when the boys came in their cars, I could see them up close and, from the looks on their faces, I don't think they could believe it, either – that they'd done this thing, this great thing – and people in Sydney cared about it! The fans knew what it meant – all these years and all that work! I was really quite emotional.'

She is, after all, an emotional person – and her love of AFL gives her a safe place to put those emotions, from exuberance to anxiety, from disappointment to simple, overwhelming human joy. Mum loves the game because it's a spectacle, and it's this quality she admires the most in her team. Mum says, 'The Swans have always been the most entertaining. Even when they've lost. When they win,' she smiles, 'it's just a bonus.'

INVISIBLE SPEARS

Ellen van Neerven

A stadium can hold the most sound
drowning out the bora ring
mudding the lines we needed to know
where we're going
now it's a clusterfuck to get the train home
flip up seats and overflowing beer
the rude odour of tomato sauce
and the black faces they never show on TV
the team with the most blackfullas
they don't want to win
the commentator's curse
the tiddling fear
of invisible spears
we can't score goals
on this sacred land
celebrated as animals

GI doing the goanna, yeah
but not people
with military intelligence
you don't want us protecting
our land like the Maori
that means it was our land to protect
we don't need
a haka of whitefullas
just let us resist.

FAMILY TIES

Stephanie Holt

'But I thought you barracked for Collingwood!' they say to me.

'But aren't you St Kilda?' they ask my husband.

It's an elementary and revealing mistake – to assume that if we share a passion for the game, Chris and I must share a team. As deep as it is arbitrary, one's footy allegiance is neither a casual accommodation nor a deal-breaker. For every family united in fandom, every couple drawn together by a shared love of a team, every fan who's converted a nonbelieving loved one, there's a family like ours, a mixed marriage.

In fact, our pairing mimics my own parents': a cerebral father more enamoured of the game itself than sharing his dad's exuberant passion for the Donboys; a one-eyed, dyed-in-the-wool mother taking her own father's quiet Collingwood commitment to another level. Just as both were grounded in the church, but Dad's Baptist, Mum's Anglican, and both came from Preston, but he West, she East, so both loved football, but followed different teams. Who knows? Perhaps that small difference added a frisson to their relationship, one I was too busy jousting with my twin brother to notice.

Our grandfathers – one given to big gestures, the other to gentle prompts – bid early for my brother's soul. One was still savouring a not-too-distant premiership; the other still smarting from the narrowest grand final loss. And so an Essendon jumper trumped a Collingwood beanie, and the rest is history. Perhaps the twin sister in the shadows was subliminally aware of a third player in those deciders, vanquished by Essendon in '65, victorious over Collingwood in '66. I was certainly swayed by the exotic pleasures of beach and gelati and sunshine and the seductively seedy seaside where my family picnicked. And so I became, for no rational or definitively recalled reason, a Saint.

For a long time footy conspired to keep me just that little bit out of step with my nearest and dearest. A footy foundling. But there's been a wonderful compensation in a succession of Saints-going 'footy families' – less than blood, but more than convenience, part fated, part chosen. When it comes to footy I've happily turned my back on immediate family and been welcomed unquestioningly by my fellow Sainters, who expect nothing more than some company in the outer, and the freedom to indulge their Sainter selves without ridicule. Being shy in temperament, rebellious in spirit, that suited me perfectly.

My first St Kilda footy family were the next-door neighbours. A successful tradie and a young hairdresser with two little girls, they added a touch of glamour to our post-war suburban street. Our two families could hardly have been more different. Where they had an above-ground swimming pool, banana lounges, a regular spot for the esky, and a few desultory shrubs hugging their fences, we had a workshop, fruit trees, a retractable clothes-line, and a carefully cultivated native garden. But they got on well, these four young parents: Dad and Mick (though my dad, formal to a fault, was the only person in the street to use Mick's given name of Stan), who shared talk of machines and engineering, Mum with her practised schoolteacher vowels and Mary with her cheery, chatty malapropisms.

Our little street ran from an empty paddock beside an imposing biscuit factory to a line of massive pine trees in a far corner of a spread of Education Department land that housed three local schools, each with its regulation share of ovals and cricket pitches and netball courts. The high school and primary school were named for our salubrious side of High Street Road: Ashwood; the tech school distinguished by the name of the Housing Commission estate across the road: Jordanville.

For a few years there, the two families would alternate Sunday morning duties, driving a load of overdressed kids – two of ours, two of theirs – up the High Street Road hill to the red-brick Anglican church for Sunday School. More often that not, the backseat talk was of footy, more teases and barbs than informed comment. That singsong 'Wodappenedto [insert team name here]?' all kids had perfected.

And at some point a parental agreement must have been brokered. I started going to football games with the neighbours. Though my own parents would take us from time to time to sparkly new family-friendly Waverley Park, it was the neighbours who took me to the old suburban grounds with their dirt and smells and noise and crowds, the cheers and jeers erupting from the terraces and resonating around the stands. Together we watched the heroes of the mid '70s slogging through the Moorabbin mud. The sharpest memories are small and intense: the details slipped onto the scoreboard – an exotic coded language – the away games, the racing results, the constantly recalibrated scores; the cold, dank concrete of the toilets; red lemonades at a pub stop on the way home; bumping along shoulder to shoulder in the back seat of Mick's work van. Like extended family, this first footy family gave me a safe and reassuring place from which to observe an unruly world, from which to step tentatively into it. I couldn't believe my luck.

Fast-forward a few years. The girl next door was dating

one of the players and her mum, Mary, was putting blond tips in his hair to catch the cameras. Or so I heard from my mum, those footy outings by then a thing of the past.

I'd stopped going to games when I started uni. It wasn't that St Kilda seemed to have a lock on a bottom-three finish, but Saturday afternoons were now given over to a weekend job in a nursing home. I'd leave my sharehouse *du jour* – invariably smelling of dirty dishes, wet towels and stale ashtrays – for leafy Canterbury and a beautiful Queen Anne mansion that smelled of piss-soaked sheets and hospital-grade disinfectant, of lavender bags and little-old-lady talc. The intensity of live games was replaced by a soothing rumble and excited stutters and shrieks from my little trannie as I shuttled between kitchen and laundry in a blue polyester uniform. Footy became a soundtrack to washing dishes and cooking soup and vitamising vegetables, and – when the dire St Kilda of the early '80s was actually in danger of winning a game – hoping the residents wouldn't mind if I held off the afternoon tea-trolley run till half-time.

Dropping out of uni might not have done my future many favours, but it improved my footy following no end, and brought me to my next footy family.

Entering the mid '80s, St Kilda, like the nation's economy, was in a dire position and I – like any self-respecting Arts degree dropout – was working in the public service.

Unemployment was high, the old industries were dying, the toughest cases were being shuffled through a succession of government employment schemes, and Footscray's Commonwealth Employment Service office was at once dismal, bustling and fascinating. As were its staff. There were world-weary career public servants, eager young recruits, and a crew of translators who shuttled back and forth between the office and the Maribyrnong Migrant Hostel, slipping effortlessly between three, four, five languages.

Socialising was a choice between endless games of 500 in the little staffroom out back, or fifty-minutes-and-counting lunches at the pub in the sad little mall, or in one of the Vietnamese places round the corner. Newly trained and keen to fit in, I duly filled out the questionnaire for the sporadic office newsletter, only to find my reference to 'obscure' magazines changed to 'obscene'. An editorial comment noted that the two best points about this proudly bra-free feminist in her baggy sweaters and op-shop skirts were 'the ones out in front'. I prepared to grit my teeth, do my job, and remain friendless.

But, as it so often does, footy offered a small opening for deeper connections. In an inspired stretch of the truth, I'd listed the 1966 grand final as a personal highlight. It turned out my two immediate bosses and the office manager barracked for the Saints. Disbelieving comments became easy conversations became tentative invitations.

I began going to games with Kaye. She was a Level 5 to my Level 4, a supervisor to my clerk, and there were at least five years between us, but at the footy we were equals. At the games, our shared passion was enough; and in the car to and from games, our stories emerged. Kaye was half Italian, half Scottish; her father had weathered wartime internment to set up a successful concreting business in a country town. He'd added an 'o' to the end of their northern-Italian surname to give his concreting business a boost, because everyone knew Italians were good concreters, and that Italian names always ended that way. I'd listen, fascinated, as she gave her own spin to the staple stories of a wog kid in an Aussie country town.

Before long, we added a third member to our footy family, my housemate Terry, an out-and-proud uni student whose New South Wales upbringing had left him clueless about the great game. The Saints made it easier for us to convert him – this was the era of small and ferocious crowds, of slogging games and pounding losses, enlivened by the unstoppable force that was Tony Lockett. And, as Terry – a novice graphic designer – was happy to endorse, they had the best jumpers by far.

We must have seemed an odd trio, but it worked, focusing on the games, and filling dull moments with mutually enlightening anecdotes of offices and nightclubs and households, of jobs and art and activism. We kept up the footy outings, even after I moved on from the public service to become a community worker, and though we grew amicably apart, it was Terry, by then an ex-housemate, who I called a couple of seasons later to help me celebrate Plugger's landmark Brownlow night in '87.

My enduring footy family, it turned out, had been waiting for me all along, on the other side of the ground. The move to join them was gradual, one of those relationships that took shape slowly and, suddenly, was recognised for what it was, full blown.

There were three of them at first: artist Greg, architect David and art historian Chris. They'd been strangers to each other until a mutual friend, not long before, had set them up on their first footy date. I guess my Magpies-supporting boyfriend, Chris, was included on the assumption it was better to see a rival team in company than to not see any footy at all. On his urging, I was soon drifting across to join them at half-time, swapping my regular seats with Kaye and Terry beside the infamous Animal Enclosure for the sunny gravel-and-concrete terrace under the Snow Deli sign with Chris, Greg and David.

In time, my Chris found more suitable (Collingwood-supporting) footy companions, but by then I was on something more than nodding terms with Greg and David, and comfortable enough with the fluctuating, often sizable, mob that would join them. It was too hard to keep track of who fancied who, who was fucking who, who was there for the footy, and who was just along for the ride; I found most of them dauntingly cool and correspondingly aloof. But for those few hours a week, footy demanded nothing more than that we stand side by side in the outer.

Almost twenty-five years ago, Greg and David surprised me by unfurling the first of our now-traditional run-through banners at a birthday party held at the Junction Oval. 'Thirty Great Games', it read. Made of red, white and black crepe, it featured a picture of a footy and a pair of 'footy boots' – my then-trademark black winklepickers. The Saints gifted me their first finals appearance since I was a kid.

The following season was our last at Moorabbin, and Greg and David spent much of it casually attentive as I grew large and awkward with a little Sainter-to-be. Perhaps that's when I finally realised that this was a special type of friendship, one that I'd been slow to recognise. There was a deep kindness in its companionship, and – like the best of families – the somewhat arbitrary entrance requirement allowed room for curiosity, for discovery. We shared this one crazy thing, revealing ourselves at our most absurd. It was strangely liberating.

Since then, friends have come and gone, prospective partners have been tested and shown off, a new generation has been born. Some have drifted away – to parenthood, to work, to travel – only to return to the fold when the time is right, or the need greatest. Along the way, Chris and I married, with Greg his best man, and five years ago our daughter, Lydia, celebrated her eighteenth birthday with a special request: her own run-through banner, held proudly by her 'footy dads', Greg and David. Her birthday party was a small affair in an upstairs room of a local pub. Lydia was deep in exams in her final year of school, and besides, my mum, her grandma, was slowly recovering from a health crisis that had rocked us all. It was a time to quietly draw close to those who mattered most – immediate family, a few old family friends, a handful of schoolmates, and – of course – the 'footy family'. They'd shared the load of caring for a restless, wide-eyed toddler; they'd helped gently indoctrinate an intrigued child; they'd built their own treasured relationships with a girl growing through teenage tumults into adulthood.

Three grand finals in two years, falling short in them all, and then falling apart, is an exquisite kind of cruelty. But we weathered it – as families do – with tears and black humour, with steeling reminiscence and quiet togetherness, with reassuring rituals and well-tested platitudes. There *is* always next kick, next quarter, next game, next draft, next season. The team might have been struggling through a rebuild on the field, but in the outer it was business as usual. Barrack for a basket case. Latch yourself to a laughing stock. We've been there before.

My mum turned eighty this year, gathering a lifetime of firm female friends for a fancy afternoon tea to celebrate. 'I've sat Lydia next to Mary,' she told me, concerned that her granddaughter, a generation or two younger than the other guests, be looked after. Mum astonishes me by saying she doesn't remember my going to the footy with Mary's family, our one-time next-door neighbours; Lydia, delighted, tells me she heard all about it, and more, from Mary herself.

It's been almost thirty years now with my own footy family, moving from Moorabbin to Waverley to Docklands. Sometimes it feels like an orphans' Christmas up on Level 3, with the old friends and the various connections. Sometimes no quantity of carefully draped scarves or strategically deposited *Footy Records* can save enough seats, and we end up in scattered clusters, shouting quarter-by-quarter reviews over bemused fellow spectators. On other days, we're just two or three huddled next to Aisle 9.

Much is given and nothing demanded by this extended footy family. Nothing, except the requirement to stay to the final siren.

PLAY LIKE A GIRL

Kirby Bentley

I grew up playing netball. I was driven, and dedicated myself to the game in every possible way. I had to overcome major injuries to reset and reignite the passion I'd had as a younger player. But a series of family tragedies changed everything.

My family has always had challenges in life – like most families, I'm sure. It's not until you get older that you learn to understand the value of life and how precious time can be. In 2007 I was still caught up in my dream of being a national league netballer, but in March that year, my first cousin, who was more like an older brother, committed suicide. It was completely unexpected. There wasn't a letter or any hint of his troubles. It left my aunty and uncle, our whole family, absolutely shattered.

Then in June of the same year we lost our pop to cancer. As a 21-year-old, although I had lived out of home and, to an extent, had to grow up quickly, I was still quite immature. I was determined to make decisions that would not jeopardise my own life or my own goals; I was naive and, I think, selfish, without realising it.

By the time we'd worked through the passing of our loved ones a year and a half had gone by, although I could see that, as a family, we weren't completely healed. That was when we were struck by another tragedy. In January 2009 my mum's sister was murdered by her estranged husband in a domestic violence dispute. I was twenty-three.

I remember how everything changed. I completely shifted my priorities to focus on my family, to protect them, and to be there for them. For us to be there for each other.

Mum had an amazing relationship with her sister, and seeing her heartache and how it affected the person she was forced me to adjust my life too. I knew I had to become a better older sister. I wanted to build on my relationship with my two younger sisters. I had to be there for them.

So it was football that brought my middle sister and myself together. I wanted to know who she was and what she enjoyed, and that, for her, was football.

Playing football was a positive distraction, my outlet. It was probably not the best way to deal with my emotions but so much was going on after the murder – the investigation, the court case. Trying to uncover all the information leading up to that fatal moment. There were so many questions from the police, but also, as a family, for ourselves too. To this day, a lot of questions have still not been answered.

Football enabled me to build on my relationship with my sister. It offered me a whole new journey, which I am grateful for. In those first matches, I remember feeling out of my comfort zone, not knowing where to position myself or what to do. Three weeks later I was invited to state training and before I knew it I was representing Western Australia at nationals in Perth. After playing only seven games of full-contact football in my whole life, I was suddenly competing against the best players in the country.

My first game for WA was against Queensland. A very solid side physically, they were also hard-hitting. I found this out when I got my first touch and my opponent laid a strong hit on me. I remember getting up and calling out to be subbed off, deciding that this wasn't the game for me. But the coach kept me on! In fact, she placed me in the middle of the ground and said, 'Get the ball and get it to our forwards. That's all you need to do.' I loved the challenge and from then, I pushed myself to learn and improve, becoming better with each game.

Since then, I've gained more experience, and I've learnt how to involve the players around me, making the game easier. I've learnt that footy is truly a team sport, and drawing on your team's strengths is how you end up in grand finals. Which is what you play for.

I made it into my first club grand final with the East

Fremantle Sharks, playing alongside my sister. It didn't start well. By the third quarter we still hadn't scored a goal. Then I snapped one from the pocket and my sister Ashleigh slotted two to put us back into the game. It remains one of my most memorable moments.

I've always had a passion to play football, but, unfortunately back then, once you reached a certain age, girls had to choose an alternative sport. It was nothing like it is now. The opportunities girls have today are a far cry from what I experienced. The access players have to quality coaching, training venues, and opportunities to play in the biggest arenas in the country is outstanding. It's the beginning of something new and exciting. There are currently two AFL clubs with women's teams, which offer players the opportunity to represent them at the highest level. Melbourne Football Club, where the game originated, and the Western Bulldogs announced their support for women's football several years ago. Two coaches were appointed, who then selected players from a national draft to fill both squads. From there, teams were selected to represent Melbourne and the Western Bulldogs at Etihad Stadium in the inaugural match – a curtain-raiser before the AFL match, during the Women's Round in July 2013. I was selected to play for Melbourne – and we won.

I have been brought up to be an independent person. My parents always encouraged me to be who I am – respectfully. Sometimes stepping into a 'man's world' – like footy, or my day job as a fly-in fly-out 'shot firer' working with explosives in the Pilbara – can be overwhelming. Convincing some men that women are just as capable can be challenging. For women to be accepted in both these worlds, you almost need to go over and above just to 'earn' your position.

I'm driven by the challenge to prove people wrong. I enjoy working up north and I love playing football. I've found that most people are surprised by the high standard of women's football, and the skill set displayed.

There are still the 'old school' men in football who believe women should be in the kitchen – or playing netball, anyway. People are entitled to their opinions, and I know that not everyone will agree with me, or pursue the same dream and aspirations. But it's the same with anything in life.

Despite this, I believe that the diversity in footy brings people together, regardless of race, fitness, skill set or upbringing. Aussie Rules is Australia's game, and more and more, it is providing opportunities for young girls and women to play professionally. They now have a pathway to the women's league, which is fantastic for the next generation of girls. And the women who have had the chance to play in the last five to ten years have seen amazing improvements, and now provide role models for the young women.

That's something we haven't had before.

But there is still work to do. I don't feel that racism in football is particularly different to racism in society. It is still very much around in general life. It's a shame that any 'game' can realise such hatred towards people, as it did in regards to Adam Goodes. He is an outstanding role model, a massive influence for all Australians, not just Indigenous people. He has worked hard throughout his career to be a respected person and footballer. It's unfortunate that his profile has been disparaged in the last year of his career.

But AFL can bring people together. Our young Indigenous girls have an amazing opportunity in football and in life. They have the world at their feet.

As I head into the last couple of years of my career, my role has changed. I am less concerned with being the best than I am with using my experience to help and empower young girls to reach their full potential. The Kirby Bentley Cup, a development program set up by the West Australian Football Commission, has created an opportunity for young Indigenous girls to enter the AFL's women's league pathway. It's important for me to give back to the game and to encourage and empower young girls who aspire to be footballers.

Most of all, I look forward to a time when women are recognised as 'footballers' and not 'female footballers'.

STELLAR HAWKS

Alan Duffy

'This is a Hawks family, Alan,' were the words my prospective in-laws told me when I first started dating their daughter nearly six years ago. When they cornered me I'd thought they would ask the usual sort of thing: my intentions for their daughter, or if I was planning to stay in Australia. But I had completely underestimated footy in this country, the all-consuming hold it has on the loyalty and love of a nation. The implication was clear: love might conquer all, but if I didn't pick the right club to follow it would make *Romeo and Juliet* look like an arranged marriage.

I've always loved sport – rugby and rowing in particular, but to be honest I'll even watch darts. So please keep that in mind when I say my first impression of footy watching the West Coast Eagles at Subiaco Oval was that this sport was *mad*. A limb was as likely to come bouncing out of a tackle as the Sherrin, assuming the ball was even near the play, and all the while, handballs and kicks were coming in every which way. A sport without an offside rule is initially a confusing one to someone from the UK but, fortunately, I was planning to stay in Oz for a while.

I had moved to Perth to join a huge international team working on the scientific and technical challenges of the first step towards the largest telescope ever conceived, the Square Kilometer Array. It was a massive undertaking and meant I would be in Australia for several years at least. This gave me plenty of time to learn the game of AFL, which would be critical if I wanted to understand what my antipodean colleagues were talking about at lunch.

Astronomers tend to think big; billions of stars as large as our sun are clumped together as one object (a galaxy) with inconceivable distances between them. To get a sense of scale, if you placed the Sun and our nearest star (Alpha Centauri) at opposite ends of the MCG, then the giant Aaron Sandilands would be only 8.5 femtometres tall (almost exactly the radius of a gold nucleus so, yes, you could say he's the Dockers' golden boy). When I watch a game of football I'm struck by how empty the field is, with all the action in these tiny regions around players, and huge long kicks travelling the space between. For some this emptiness can be disconcerting. For me it feels just right.

In 2010 I was fortunate to meet my now fiancée, and no less fortunate to swiftly find my way to a game at one of the greatest stadiums in the world, the incredible MCG, to watch the mighty Hawks with my eventual in-laws. Finally the game of football made sense. The Hawks are known for their clinically accurate kicks that isolate the opposition, for their ability to ensure the ball finds its way to players in space, and, ultimately, through the sticks thanks to (then) Buddy Franklin or (now) Jarryd Roughead. Adding flair to the spectacle there'll be some random occasions of magic from Cyril Rioli. Perhaps, even, a specky or two.

How did I ever think this code was chaotic? There's a pattern to the sport that the best teams exhibit, a form of chess, which the scientist in me can't help but try to quantify. Just like finding galaxies, or building telescopes, these things take time, and seeing the beauty in footy took a year or so. But I've never looked back. That I've arrived at a time of historic dominance by the Hawks makes it all the easier to appreciate their uniquely elegant play, and ensures that grand final day is the highlight of the year.

Now I'm officially an Aussie I can take pleasure making sure recent arrivals to these shores choose the right footy team, too.

AS LONG AS IT ISN'T ESSENDON

Jacqui James

I was born with severe athetoid cerebral palsy. The movement and balance area in my brain was damaged due to a lack of oxygen in a traumatic birth. The 'athetoid' means I have erratic spasms in my body *all the time*. I am non-verbal. My mum knew I wasn't mentally impaired because, even from those early months, I was smiling and recognising people and objects. Against an assessment of severe mental impairment (all because I couldn't physically point to the *red* block) she continued to put up photos and pictures of family and objects on the walls so I could look and identify them using facial expressions. Mum fought for me to be integrated into a mainstream primary school. I was one of the first in Australia of my 'kind' (with such complex needs) to be integrated, so it wasn't easy. We had to fight the system all the way through to VCE and on to TAFE.

When I was seven, Mum bought me a Bulldog soft toy dressed in the team uniform. She is a keen Doggies supporter like her father. The toy was a perfect size for me to cuddle in bed and had big enough ears to bite into so I could drag it onto my chest. I don't have fine motor control so grabbing objects with my hands takes forever. But I learnt very early that if there's a will, there's a way. (The little Bulldog is now safely kept in a waterproof tub in our shed with my beloved Cabbage Patch doll, Jeanette.)

Dad is a boastful Geelong supporter who broke into 'We are Geelong, the greatest team of all' at every chance he got. He was a football player himself in his teenage years. It's amusing watching a televised match with him; he plays out the entire game alongside the players. He ducks, kicks and takes a specky all while sitting down. You could be choking and trying to get his attention but he wouldn't notice. So I worked out early that I had to make a choice. The Bulldogs won.

Then came the scarf and beanie I wore proudly during my primary and secondary school years. I wasn't very fussed with AFL at first. Don't get me wrong – I loved the Doggies and knew some of the players' names, such as Tony Liberatore, Stephen Wallis and the absolute legend Simon Beasley. I remember my friends and I feeling gooey over Essendon's Gavin Wanganeen and, I'm very embarrassed to admit this, James Hird (what an interesting character he's turned out to be). But it wasn't until 1998 when I first met my great friend Francis that I began to care whether or not the Doggies won. In 2000, after Docklands Stadium was only just built, Francis decided to take me to my very first footy match. What would have been an exhilarating experience turned into a war with the stadium. We didn't realise all the disabled car parks are underground, and my 2.4 metre–high commuter van wouldn't fit. We had to park outside the ground instead. It was very painful and difficult, travelling all that way. Francis (and my nan) phoned Neil Mitchell from 3AW and spoke live on-air after the game. They were all disgusted with the lack of disabled car parks for high-roofed vans, even though Docklands was a brand-new establishment. (Even today, there are still none available.)

The game, however, was incredible. Western Bulldogs lost to Essendon, 81 to 144. I never forgave Essendon though, especially after Francis draped a Dons scarf on me for a photo.

In September that year the back of my useless wheelchair collapsed. I fell backwards, my headrest ending up on the floor and my back hyper-extended. I now have a back injury with chronic nerve pain including sciatica (I call it Mr Shitty) and sharp, zapping twinges all through my body. Due to this chronic pain, I haven't gone to a footy match for several years.

The last match I attended was the Pink Lady Match at the MCG a few years ago. I went with Mum (a breast cancer survivor) and my brother. It took a lot of effort and pain to get there but it was one of the most memorable moments of my life. Sitting among the brave survivors and people celebrating and remembering their loved ones was highly emotional and moving.

So it was wonderful to discover Balloon Football on the internet. When I first heard of its existence I thought how cool it was for people who have the desire to play football to do so, even though they might be in a wheelchair. I've always known it doesn't matter how much or how little your physical capabilities are. I often say how my brain is always willing, but my body lets me down. I'd love to watch when I can.

Balloon Football is a modified version of Aussie Rules and is played while the AFL season is running. There are local teams including Victorian State, Bendigo, Melbourne and Geelong. They all battle for a Perpetual Trophy every year. The aim is the same as in AFL: to score the most points. Teamwork and sportsmanship are the two main attributes of the sport. I spoke to Cameron West, one of the founders of Balloon Football, who has been playing the game for around twenty years. He has cerebral palsy and plays using his electric wheelchair. He also barracks for the Blues. He is clearly proud of the game and describes its fast pace. When I ask about the physicality involved, he says,

'It can be dangerous if you are going backwards and you have your eye on the ball. You could hit someone and cause injury. It's part of the rules for players not to travel backwards during play. It is better for me if I have a student driving my chair during the game.'

Involving able-bodied students in the matches is a great aspect of Balloon Football – whether it is to push people in wheelchairs around the court or to umpire matches. This involvement of students promotes education and acceptance of peoples' disabilities which, in turn, helps fight the stigma around disability. I can clearly see the promise of the game. I hope there's a groundswell of supporters, players and volunteers. I may not play any time soon, but I'll be sure to wear a scarf. As long as it isn't in Essendon colours.

Q&A

Peta Searle

When did AFL first get a hold of you?

My parents were passionate Saints supporters. From the moment I was brought home from the hospital they took me to Moorabbin in my bassinet. I spent my childhood sliding down the concrete pillars in the outer, riding cardboard boxes down the hill and kicking the footy on the oval after the game until dark. Then I would make my way up to the social rooms where Trevor Barker would carry me around on his shoulders. My love for the game and the Saints, like many kids, was part of every Saturday afternoon.

When was the first moment you thought your insights and skills could help others?

As a Physical Education teacher I worked with many teams.

There was a specific moment when I was supervising the Year 7 girls' hockey team: there was this girl who was not the most skilful person, and I said to her, 'If you just stand near the post when it deflects off the goalkeeper you'll be able to tap it in.' Then, wow! She did it. On the sidelines I jumped with excitement. I was so elated for her, scoring her first goal. I remember the joy I felt for her achievement and, at the time, I realised it was more than I was getting out of my own participation and achievements at a high level. It was at that moment I knew I wanted to coach. I wanted to help other people achieve their goals, grow as people, and experience the richness that being involved in sport brings.

You've been 'the first' many times, including the first woman to coach in the VFL and now the first and only female coach at the AFL level. While you were accomplishing these firsts, did you feel pressure to prove yourself?

The nature of coaching inevitably involves pressure, so it's something you learn to absorb and use to make yourself better. When I first got the job at Port Melbourne I felt like I had to prove myself. Especially because, at VFL games, anyone is free to come onto the ground and listen to you speak. Gary Ayres always had a multitude of people listening to him, and I would have the next largest group. People wanted to see if this chick knew what she was talking about. After some quick evaluation I started to think, *Stop trying to impress and just be impressive!* To be impressive I just had to believe in myself and do my job. When I got back to that, I served the players better and became a better coach. There's always going to be external pressure being the first female coach but as I am my own biggest critic, I probably place the most pressure on myself – not just to achieve and do well, but to always get better.

What attributes does a good coach have?

The goal of a great coach is to guide, inspire and empower people to achieve their full potential as players and as people, by getting them to believe in themselves, and then to stretch the limits of their beliefs. Great coaches are emotionally mature, keenly self-aware, and have the ability to manage their emotions. They are able to create substantial relationships with others, are empathetic and tuned in to their players' feelings. They must have a genuine care and interest in all of their players and support team. But most of all they coach the person, not the player. Needless to say, a great coach will also possess exceptional communication skills. An effective coach is able to set defined goals, express these goals and ideas clearly to players, give direct feedback, reinforce key messages and acknowledge success. A coach should be a compassionate listener who welcomes player comments, questions and feedback, and creates an emotionally safe learning environment, crucial for optimal learning and peak performance. They are honest, conduct themselves with integrity and must be strong role models, continually challenging themselves to evolve and grow. They are passionate about what they do, and love the game.

Was anything or anyone holding you back? Conversely, was anyone championing you?

I've never felt like there were things holding me back, because there was always something I could do to change it. However there are certainly things that make it more difficult. For example, simply navigating day-to-day life as a single parent – both logistically and financially – is difficult. But that's life and that's reality for many people. At times I have come across male coaches who have been unsure how to accept me in what they perceive as their space, but, overall, the support has been overwhelming.

I would not have made it here without this support. For that I owe a lot to Gary Ayres and Sam Lane. Gary not only gave me a break, appointing me Assistant Coach at Port Melbourne, but, also, his ability to mentor and develop me as a coach and his continued support has been remarkable. Also, you need someone with influence who believes in you to tell your story, and (Fairfax journalist) Sam Lane has been that person for me. She continually championed my cause – and the cause of many women in the industry – in the public eye until finally it was heard. She is a journalist who has built a philosophy around wanting to help people – and not just wanting to report – which is one of the many factors that make her an outstanding journalist and an even better person. My life has been enriched because of her.

Who were your main mentors at any stage in your career (football or otherwise)?

When I played football I didn't have any female football role models to look up to. My heroes were males: Trevor Barker and Nathan Burke. It's exciting for young girls today wanting to play the game to have the likes of Daisy Pearce and Katie Brennan to look up to. It has been a positive step forward in demonstrating that girls can achieve their dreams and goals too.

I have been very lucky to have been surrounded by and brought up by two beautiful women: my grandma and my mother. Both have been exemplary in demonstrating work ethic, resilience and determination, and have provided me with the essential foundations required to succeed and grow.

How far has footy got to go as far as women are concerned? What would you like to see change/develop?

I think the involvement of women in football is tracking in the right way. It's just a matter of time before we see more female coaches at AFL clubs. I would like to think at some stage a woman could be a head coach. In terms of women playing the game, ultimately I would like them to have equal recognition playing at all levels. To have an equal playing field, in terms of respect – for who they are and what they bring to the game. They are highly talented, dedicated and extraordinary women who deserve as much respect and recognition as their male counterparts.

Losing

EMMA
Not

FELICITY

EMMA
HOLDING THE

LUCY
donkey

EMMA

KATE
FUCK

FELICITY

EMMA
Prague will get a team before Tasmania.

PUBLICATION DETAILS

Stan Grant's 'I Can Tell You How Adam Goodes Feels. Every Indigenous Person Has Felt It' appeared in the *Guardian*, 30 July 2015. Copyright Guardian News & Media Ltd 2015.

Sam Pang and Brendan Murray's 'Doull's Gold' appeared in the *Age*, 28 May 2005.

Peter Rose's 'Operamanes' appeared in *The House of Vitriol*, Picador, Sydney, 1990.

Ellen van Neervan's 'Invisible Spears' appeared in *Overland*, Spring 2015, issue 220.

NOTES ON CONTRIBUTORS

EDITORS

Nicole Hayes' debut release, *The Whole of My World* (2013), is a young adult novel and the first 'footy novel' to feature a teenage girl. It was longlisted for the 2014 Gold Inky and shortlisted for the 2014 YABBAs. Her second novel, *One True Thing* (2015), was awarded the 2015 Children's Peace Literature Award. She bleeds Brown and Gold, which you'd know if you followed her on Twitter: @nichmelbourne.

Alicia Sometimes is a writer, poet, broadcaster and musician. She was a 3RRR Breakfaster and was on Aural Text for fourteen years. She is a regular guest on 774 and Radio National, was editor of the national literary journal *Going Down Swinging* for seven years and has appeared in ABC TV's Sunday Arts and ABC News Breakfast. She is also the writer and director of the science-poetry planetarium show *Elemental*. Alicia is a mad Hawks supporter. Twitter: @aliciasometimes.

CONTRIBUTORS

Van Badham is a writer, activist and occasional broadcaster. One of Australia's most controversial social commentators, she writes a weekly column for *Guardian Australia*. She is the recipient of three Premier's awards for her work as a theatremaker; her stage work has been translated into several languages and performed all over the world. A proud alumnus of the University of Wollongong, Van, like her mother before her, has the red and white heart of a Swan.

Kirby Bentley is a premiership AFL player and Debbie Lee Medallist who has represented WA, the Indigenous Yorga Team and the Melbourne Football Club, and is an All-Australian team member. Named after her, the Kirby Bentley Cup is a football development program for Aboriginal girls. She inherited her love for the Eagles from her pop and her dad, diehard fans who told her, 'Barrack for the Eagles or move out.'

Tony Birch's most recent book is *Ghost River* (UQP, 2015). He is currently the inaugural Bruce McGuinness Research Fellow at Victoria University. As a rugged half-back flanker he rose to the dizzy heights of 'The Most Determined' trophy winner for East Hawthorn Under-5s. In presenting the award his coach made the now-immortalised remark, 'This boy would eat a football rather than let his opponent get a touch.'

Honey Brown is the author of six critically acclaimed novels. In her late twenties she was involved in a farm accident, resulting in a spinal injury. This life-changing event led to a focus on writing. A Collingwood girl, she comes from a family tree with territorial Magpies perched on every Black and White branch.

Maxine Beneba Clarke is an Australian writer of Afro-Caribbean descent. She is the author of *Foreign Soil*, which won the 2015 ABIA award for Literary Fiction Book of the Year, and the 2015 Indie Award for debut fiction. Her memoir, *The Hate Race*, and her first picture book, *The Patchwork Bike*, are forthcoming in 2016. She can't kick a footy to save herself.

Sophie Cunningham is the author of four books, including *Melbourne* (2011) and *Warning: The Story of Cyclone Tracy* (2014). She is a former editor of *Meanjin*, and former Chair of the Literature Board of the Australia Council. She is mad for the Cats.

Catherine Deveny is a comedian, writer and speaker. She has published over 1000 columns in *The Age*, is the author of seven books, has been on ABC's *Q&A* five times, and is a Melbourne International Comedy Festival regular. She is the creator of The Gunnas Writing Masterclass, co-founder of Pushy Women and the Supreme Being of The Atheist Kibbutz. Feminist, enthusiast, dyslexic and maverick.

Demet Divaroren is a Melbourne-based writer, editor and creative writing teacher. She is the co-editor of *Coming of Age: Growing up Muslim in Australia*. Demet is a passionate Western Bulldog who once appeared on a billboard alongside her favourite player, Chris Grant.

Dr Alan Duffy is an astronomer at Swinburne University who creates baby universes on powerful supercomputers to learn more about the nature of dark matter. He is often seen on TV or heard on radio getting way too excited about science. He became a Hawks fan in 2010, soon after arriving in Australia.

Stan Grant is of the Wiradjuri and Kamilaroi nations of New South Wales. Stan is an award-winning journalist and is currently Indigenous Editor for the *Guardian Australia*, Managing Editor for National Indigenous Television and International Editor for Sky News. In 2015 he won a

Walkley Award for his columns for the *Guardian*. He barracks for the Rabbitohs.

Leila Gurruwiwi is a TV presenter on *The Marngrook Footy Show* and a Deadly Sista Girlz mentor for The Wirrpanda Foundation. Leila has appeared on radio, emceed at many events and had acting roles in *Team of Life*, *The Secret River* and *Glitch*. Leila is passionate about her own Yolngu culture and learning about other Indigenous Australian cultures as well as the other wonderful cultures that share Australia. Leila loves heading over the West Gate Bridge to watch the Western Bulldogs do their thing!

Stephanie Holt is a Saints tragic who writes occasionally about football and other passions (books, art, feminism) while working as a freelance editor, teacher and program coordinator with RMIT's Professional Writing and Editing programs. She also has a soft spot for the Castlemaine Magpies and the Boston Lady Demons.

Jacqui James is a music journalist, poet and children's author. She was born with severe Athetoid Cerebral Palsy, which is a physical disability. She's unable to speak so she communicates by computer. People say she talks more than some verbal people! She's also a proud Western Bulldogs supporter.

Rebecca Lim is the author of sixteen books for children and young adult readers, including *The Astrologer's Daughter*. A finalist for the Prime Minister's Literary Award, Davitt Award and Aurealis Award for YA, Rebecca's work has also been longlisted for the Gold Inky, the David Gemmell Legend Award and the CBCA Book of the Year Award for Older Readers. Rebecca officially barracks for the Carlton Football Club but retains a soft spot for the Mighty Hawks.

Brendan Murray is a teacher who in 2009 received the inaugural Australian Government Closing the Gap Award for strengthening partnerships between Indigenous and non-Indigenous Australians, and was also awarded the Victorian Education Department's Secondary Teacher of the Year. He played Reserves for Collingwood and still barracks for them. Just.

Bev O'Connor is a journalist and broadcaster with over twenty years experience, predominantly with the ABC. Over her career she has covered politics, business and sport. This stood her in good stead when she became the first female vice president of an AFL club, Melbourne, which is one of the most successful clubs in history (just not recent history).

Sam Pang is a comedian who barracks for Carlton but played Under-19s for Collingwood. He's a much better supporter than he was player.

Angela Pippos is a journalist, TV presenter, radio personality, author and former sports anchor on the ABC TV News. She is the author of *The Goddess Advantage: One Year in the Life of a Football*, and a new book that examines the relationship between sport and sexism in Australia. The last eleven minutes of the 1997 preliminary final were the best eleven minutes of her life until the birth of her son in 2013.

Alice Pung and **Nick Cadle** are writers from Melbourne. Alice's books include *Unpolished Gem*, *Her Father's Daughter* and *Laurinda*, as well as the Marly books from the *Our Australian Girl* series. Nick has written about football for *Ted Sports* and *The Footy Almanac Online*. Alice supports the Western Bulldogs, Nick supports Essendon and their baby, Leo, gets to choose when he is old enough.

Erin Riley is a sometimes-writer who, despite only being a footy fan for twelve years, has already seen her glorious Sydney Swans play in four grand finals. She tries hard not to gloat about this, but fails often.

Chelsea Roffey is an Aussie rules tragic-turned-goal umpire and the first woman to officiate in an AFL grand final. A journalist and avid traveller, she has been an invited guest of APEC at its women's leadership forum in Beijing and toured the world on a Churchill Fellowship exploring social change that enables girls to be the authors of their own lives. Her favourite party trick is signalling a goal in social situations. Not.

Peter Rose has published six collections of poetry, most recently *The Subject of Feeling* (UWA Publishing, 2015). His family memoir, *Rose Boys* (2001), covers his childhood at Collingwood, where his father, Bob Rose, was a player and coach.

Peta Searle was appointed St Kilda Football Club Development Coach in early 2014, becoming the first female coach in the AFL. Previously, she was Port Melbourne's assistant coach in their 2012 VFL title defence and head coach for the Western Bulldogs Women's team in the AFL's first exhibition match. Peta grew up barracking for the Saints.

Anna Spargo-Ryan inherited two things from her dad: short legs, and a one-eyed love of the Geelong Football Club. She writes for publications like *Overland*, *The Guardian*, *Seizure*, *Kill Your Darlings* and others. Her first novel is forthcoming from Picador but includes neither football nor cats.

Miriam Sved's debut novel, *Game Day* (Picador 2014), is set in and around a Victorian AFL club. She lives in Melbourne and is working on her next book, and her life still revolves around the footy season whether she likes it or not.

A long time ago before she had three children, **Jacqueline Tomlins** published two non-fiction books. These days she writes to advocate change for the LGBTIQ community. She writes articles for the gay and mainstream press, a highly regarded blog and, most recently, a resource kit for rainbow families. She co-founded the Australian Equality Party with Jason Tuazon-McCheyne to promote fairness, human rights and equality in Australian politics. Oh! And Go Hawks!

Christos Tsiolkas is an award-winning Australian author of five novels, including *The Slap* and *Barracuda*. Christos is also a playwright, essayist and film critic. He barracks for the Tigers in footy, the Victory in Aussie soccer and AEK in the Greek Football League.

Jason Tuazon-McCheyne is a longtime supporter of marriage equality and the rights of same-sex families, and is passionate about tackling homophobia in sport. He is the leader of the Australian Equality Party, and founding member of the Purple Bombers, the Essendon Football Club's LGBTI-friendly cheer squad.

Ellen van Neerven is a proud Queenslander – a young Yugambeh woman born in Brisbane. She is the author of the award-winning *Heat and Light* (UQP, 2014). She barracks for the North Queensland Cowboys.

ACKNOWLEDGEMENTS

This book emerged out of our shared love of footy and books – the very thing that brought us together in the first place. While the idea came naturally and seamlessly, as with all great ideas, the hard part was in the execution. Quite simply, we couldn't have pulled it off without the help of the following people:

Our brilliant team at Black Inc.: Caitlin Yates, Julian Welch and Elisabeth Young for their enthusiasm and support from the start, and our editor extraordinaire, Jo Rosenberg, who guided us through this tricky and exciting first journey into editorial collaboration, and whose sharp pen and keen eye brought out the best in all of our stories. Thank you, Jo. Thanks also to Oslo Davis for his incredible cover.

Early on we drew on the talents of a range of literary folk, including Catherine Harris, Martin Flanagan, Angela

Savage and Samuel Wagan Watson, as well as Elizabeth Troyeur, Stacey Gadway and Emma Van Der Aa. We tested the patience and generosity of our friends every time we drifted off mid-conversation to add a name or propose a new idea while compiling this book, and our families who had to listen to us rabbit on about looming deadlines and author bios for the duration.

A huge thank you to our dear footy friends, and fellow Hawk fans, Emma Race, Lucy Race, Felicity Race, and Kate Seear, whose IMs and DMs have kept us entertained and reassured of our sanity throughout this most excellent of footy seasons, while also providing the inspiration we needed for 'The Warm Up', 'The Game' and 'Losing'. Stay crazy, our fine Hawk friends.

Most of all, we'd like to thank our contributors – for opening their hearts and minds to the subject, for hitting deadlines, and for pushing themselves that little bit harder to strike the perfect pitch. They're all champions, but in the end, football is the real winner.